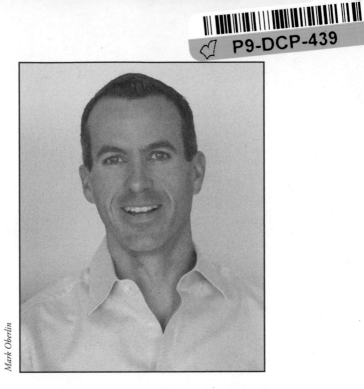

Mark Oberlin

**CYD ZEIGLER** is one of the world's foremost experts on LGBT issues in sports. Along with his *Outsports* cofounder Jim Buzinski, Zeigler has written more coming-out stories of LGBT people—in sports or any other arena—than any journalist in America. These stories have included former NBA player John Amaechi, former NFL prospect Wade Davis, NFL hopeful Michael Sam, and NCAA basketball player Derrick Gordon, in addition to countless other athletes and coaches in high school, college, and pro sports. Zeigler also cofounded the Sports Equality Foundation, which helps fund the cycle of LGBT people coming out and being out in sports. He appears regularly on ESPN, and in the *New York Times* and *USA Today*, and provides expertise on LGBT sports issues for countless other media outlets including *Sports Illustrated*, CNN, the *Los Angeles Times*, and NPR. He is a former high school athlete, still holding school track-and-field records twenty-five years later. A graduate of Stanford University, Zeigler lives in Los Angeles with his husband and two cats.

# FAIR PLAY

HOW LGBT ATHLETES ARE CLAIMING THEIR RIGHTFUL PLACE IN SPORTS

## BY CYD ZEIGLER

Published by Akashic Books
©2016 Cyd Zeigler

ISBN: 978-1-61775-447-0
Library of Congress Control Number: 2015954114

First printing

*Edge of Sports*
c/o Akashic Books
Twitter: @AkashicBooks
Facebook: AkashicBooks
E-mail: info@akashicbooks.com
Website: www.akashicbooks.com

**ALSO FROM EDGE OF SPORTS BOOKS
(CURATED BY DAVE ZIRIN)**

*Chasing Water: Elegy of an Olympian*
by Anthony Ervin & Constantine Markides

*You Throw Like a Girl*
by Don McPherson
(forthcoming)

*Unsportsmanlike Conduct:
College Football and the Politics of Rape*
by Jessica Luther
(forthcoming)

## ACKNOWLEDGMENTS

I have been blessed to receive some lovely compliments from people about the work I've done with LGBT athletes and coaches over the years. My response to that is always the same: I'm doing my part just like everybody else.

That's sometimes taken as feigned humility, but it's actually a philosophy of life that stems straight from sports. No athlete or coach can do anything by herself. It takes an entire team to beat your rivals and win the day.

This is remarkably true of the LGBT sports movement. We have only gotten to where we are today—with people finding the strength to be themselves and their teammates having the heart to support them—because of countless folks who have contributed their time, sweat, and voices to the cause.

While this book focuses largely on the last fifteen years, the work done to get to what you might call the "modern LGBT sports movement" is the foundation upon which everything has moved so quickly. Until 2000 there were precious few voices talking about the need for change.

An incredibly powerful voice for social change, not just for LGBT athletes but across sports, has been Dave Zirin. It's because of Dave that you're reading this book. Later on I'll talk about the role of "allies" in a social justice movement. I don't know any straight man (except probably Patrick Burke) who understands this better than Dave, the champion of this book and the person who got it published (with a nod to Johnny Temple of Akashic Books who has embraced the project from the first e-mail).

I know my voice would not exist in this movement if it weren't for Jim Buzinski. When I first came out in the summer of 1996, I met Jim weeks later. Then a sports editor for the *Long Beach Press-Telegram*, he helped shape my image of gay men as a part of the sports world, not separate from it. Jim, a lifelong athlete and sports fan, was a lifeline between my "former" and "future" selves. Without his friendship and mentorship, we would not have started *Outsports*, I would not have written this book, and the sports world would not be the largely welcoming place it is today for LGBT people.

It was very early on in our days running *Outsports* that I learned of the decades-long work of three women: Pat Griffin, Helen Carroll, and Sue Rankin. While men have started catching up in the fight for LGBT equality in sports, these three women were ahead of the curve demanding equality for us and educating people in sports on how we can get there. All of them successful athletes or coaches, they have felt both the heartbreak and heartwarming success of LGBT sports folks for longer than virtually anyone else in this movement. The work that comes today stands on the foundation they helped build.

Yet the father of this movement, the person who publicly gave birth to the idea that gay people can be successful and accepted in sports from high school to the pros, is Dave Kopay. A former NFL running back who played for Vince Lombardi and came out publicly in 1975 shortly after his retirement, Dave was living a comfortable life when he decided to step into the light and share his truth. He didn't have to, yet at the same time he needed to. That dynamic, along with his powerful demonstration of courage, set the benchmark for so many other athletes and nonathletes who would come out after him. To call Dave a "trailblazer" lifts the definition of the word.

There are so many other incredible people who have taught me life lessons about courage, strength, and the need to lift up other people. This section of the book could go on for twenty pages—thankfully, I'm able to talk about many of these folks over the next dozen chapters.

Yet I'd be remiss without mentioning my husband, Dan Pinar. For millennia the idea of marrying someone you love (or are assigned to at birth) has been an assumed societal right or responsibility. Over the course of the fifteen years covered in this book, my ability to marry the person I love has transformed. Dan has been in my life virtually that entire time, never wavering in his support for the work Jim and I do in lifting up the voices and spirits of other people. You would not be reading this book without the support of the most important person in the world to me—my husband Dan.

# Table of Contents

# INTRODUCTION
## *Wearing Two Hats*

*"Your purpose in life* is simply to leave the world a better place than you found it."

That's the advice my mother gave me when I was just entering my teens, a kid like so many struggling with his identity. She had no doubt heard it from someone else who assuredly had heard it from someone else. It's a platitude straight off one of those posters with a waterfall in the background. But as a kid it struck me as particularly true. If I wasn't living my life for someone else, then what the hell was the point of living at all?

I've worked for some incredibly powerful companies in my life, from the Walt Disney Company to Morgan Stanley. I currently have the pleasure of being part of Vox Media, a fast-growing former start-up that looks to dominate the online media landscape. I've met the president of the United States and had dinner with some of the most powerful people in Hollywood.

Yet it's the young LGBT athletes who have left the most lasting impressions on me.

When I first talked with Conner Mertens he was a scared kid trying to find his way on the Willamette University football team. Identifying as bisexual, he knew he was different, but inside him was a desire to express his true self despite what his teammates might think. When he finally came out to his football brethren and to the world—through a story I wrote for

*Outsports*—he found acceptance and love he hadn't fathomed.

Dalton Maldonado was a high school basketball player in Kentucky. When he was forced out of the closet by an opposing team from Lexington, they (allegedly, of course) tried to attack him, then chased his school bus. Still, Maldonado's rural Kentucky teammates stuck by his side all the way to the state playoffs.

Stephen Alexander was a standout player for his girls high school basketball team before transitioning. He returned to his rural Rhode Island high school as a boys coach in several different sports, including baseball and tennis. Despite his well-documented past as a female athlete, Alexander found acceptance from the people in his conservative hometown.

The last decade has been colored in rainbows by young athletes like these brave youth who dared to be themselves. While so many in the media focus heavily on professional athletes, it's these young LGBT athletes—growing in number—who have shown us the face of the movement.

It wasn't always this way. LGBT people in sports have long believed they didn't belong—particularly gay men and trans people. A sense of belonging in sports still doesn't exist for countless people—including all genders—struggling to find their identities in this world.

Even so, we have made so many incredible strides for LGBT athletes in the last fifteen years. In 1999, when Jim Buzinski and I started *Outsports*, gay athletes were marginalized by people in sports as well as by members of the gay community. Sports were no place for people like me, a message that was reinforced daily by both straight athletes on the basketball court and gay men in West Hollywood.

"Oh, you like sports?" I would routinely hear from gay men I met in the late nineties. "How butch of you."

That "butch" label was designed to marginalize me and people like me. We had to be putting on an act with our professed love of sports—uncomfortable with our sexual orientation and the mandatory embrace of Broadway show tunes. I was deemed a "self-loathing" gay man because I didn't check all the stereotypical boxes. Sports and the gay community? Outside of Rosie O'Donnell playing softball, they simply didn't mix.

Today those two disparate worlds have merged.

I was recently at an "LGBT Pride Night" hosted by the Los Angeles Dodgers. Just fifteen years earlier, security at Dodgers Stadium had ejected two lesbian fans for kissing one another during a game.

At the Pride Night in 2015, Ty Herndon, an openly gay country singer, sang the national anthem. The attendance of four prominent LGBT people—including MLB Inclusion Ambassador Billy Bean and Magic Johnson's son EJ—was highlighted on the field before the game. The Dodgers had even created a special Pride Night margarita (at fourteen dollars hardly a deal, but it was the thought that counted) and used gay pop singer Lance Bass to introduce the players before the game, projecting rainbow flags around the stadium as fans filed into their seats. The entire evening was orchestrated by team executive Erik Braverman, who would come out publicly via *Outsports* months later.

That's a lot of gay, a sincere effort by the team to make LGBT people feel comfortable at Dodgers Stadium. When I talked to the team's chief marketing officer, Lon Rosen, he put the night in perspective: "We've moved past the past. We need to make sure all of our fans know they are welcome and embraced."

That very afternoon I had been exchanging messages with two athletes, one a high school wrestler in Massachusetts and the other a college swimmer in Oklahoma. Both of them were struggling with their sexual orientation, trying to find their place in the world amidst concerns about their teams and their families. "I'm not totally out about my identity due to conservative friends and family I have," the swimmer from Oklahoma told me.

While it might be easy to compartmentalize this athlete's experience to the plains states, that's a big mistake. There are about 150 teams in the Big Five men's sports leagues in America. Every major city in the country—and many midsized and smaller cities—calls one of them home. Of all those teams, only one—the Los Angeles Galaxy soccer team—has an out gay male athlete. Despite the Dodgers' lovely outreach that has been mirrored by MLB teams in Philadelphia, Chicago, San Francisco, and others, not one athlete in major league men's professional sports is out, other than MLS' Robbie Rogers. Not one more.

I am driven every day to help those athletes and coaches who feel confined to the closet. It is now their time to be free.

I remember struggling as a young gay athlete. The soccer, hockey, and basketball players at Harwich High School in Massachusetts could tell that I was gay since we were in elementary school. They teased me mercilessly. I was slammed against lockers, called "faggot," and worse. It happened every day. I learned at a young age that sports were no place for a gay kid.

Yet something unexpected happened my sophomore year in high school: I led my track team in scoring—I was the team MVP. On the precipice of setting school records, the "faggot" taunts faded into the distance. I won major athletic awards before any of my "jock" classmates, all because I was faster than anybody else and worked diligently to get even faster. I learned then that sports hold a uniquely powerful position to shift our culture in ways that nothing else—not news media nor politics nor the arts—could dream. Sports, driven by an insatiable appetite for victory, evened the playing field for LGBT people.

When we started *Outsports* I had an inkling of what we were doing. The gay community (that's what we called it then) and the sports world had never been brought together like we intended. Sure, there had been gay sports leagues, but they were sports ghettos in the gay community that nary a mainstream sports figure would venture into. We intended to create something different, where the two worlds would collide.

Our ability to bridge the divide became most powerfully apparent to me when I attended the 2012 NFLPA Rookie Premiere event, a flag football game and celebrity party celebrating the NFL's rookie class. While Andrew Luck eluded me, I got to speak with many of the other incoming rookies—and some of the league's retired veterans—about the acceptance of a gay teammate. They couldn't have been more warm and responsive to my questions. I attended that event two years in a row and spoke with some wonderful incoming NFL rookies, like Doug Martin, Robert Griffin III, and Landry Jones.

Yet both years I was stopped and questioned by representatives of the NFLPA. They wanted to know why I was asking questions about gay athletes. The first year the NFLPA rep actually told me to stop asking the questions, but former Packers running back Ahman Green told the guy—in the nicest of terms—to fuck off. The second year I attended the event, in 2013, an NFLPA spokesperson stopped me after several of my interviews; he had been listening to my questions about having gay teammates.

"Some people are uncomfortable with the questions you're asking," he said to me. "We'd like you to ask the athletes' permission before asking them any questions."

No one has professionally insulted me so deeply as the NFLPA did those two days. Truly. I have been denied interviews—I can handle that. When former NFL player and coach Tony Dungy declined to be interviewed for this book, it was no surprise. In this case, the NFLPA had granted me a credential that day but thought their newest members couldn't handle a couple questions about having a gay teammate. In 2013. At that time, six NFL teams represented states that had legalized same-sex marriage; two years later, the United States Supreme Court would legalize marriage equality nationally. Yet the NFLPA felt innocuous questions about gay teammates might be out of bounds. The athletes I spoke to were totally cool and answered my questions, yet the guys in suits were uncomfortable. (They blamed it on complaints from the athletes, but I don't buy it.)

To be clear, the NFLPA has in the last four years been helpful and welcoming to me and to initiatives intended to combat homophobia. Yet on those days, that dynamic—the fear of "the questions"—was eye-opening. I redoubled my dedication to dismantling the fear and outward homophobia in sports that I felt those two days.

Since then, both Jim and I have embraced the wearing of two hats in this LGBT sports movement.

Sometimes I am an advocate for LGBT athletes. When Michael Sam's publicist Howard Bragman came to me in January 2014 looking for help, I responded with the best advice I could offer to make the NFL prospect's public coming-out as smooth and impactful as possible. I wasn't out to get the story, I didn't try to scoop the *New York Times* or *ESPN*. All I focused on was providing the best possible advice to Michael and his team. From a media perspective it was a home run.

Other times I am a journalist looking to get the story. When Bragman said I could write a behind-the-scenes feature on Sam's coming-out—as I would be privy to information unknown to *ESPN* and the *Times*—I jumped at the chance. My advocacy, and prioritizing the welfare of the athlete, had led me to one of the biggest stories of my career. It wasn't the first or last time that happened.

But mostly I have been in a continuous struggle to balance the two worlds in which I came of age: sports and the gay community.

We have made so many strides in the last fifteen years, but it's always the final stretch that is the most difficult. In 2014 the average NFL team scored a touchdown in the red zone—the last stage of their drives down the gridiron—only 50 percent of the time. A 50 percent success rate isn't going to cut it for the LGBT sports movement. We have to be better than NFL teams in the red zone. With the crushing rates at which LGBT youth attempt suicide, we can't succeed just 50 percent of the time. We have to win it all. Now.

With this book I hope to shed some light on the truths about LGBT athletes—the powerful acceptance so many of them have faced, and the limited yet enduring scope of rejection by people in power. The book focuses on men, in large part because of my own experiences as a gay man in sports, and in part because most of the athletes and coaches I've worked with through *Outsports* have been men. The stories and struggles of men and women—whether LGBT or not—in sports raise many different issues. While this book focuses more on the men, the rich history of lesbians in sports, along with other women's issues, will also be addressed.

Regardless of gender, LGBT athletes have loving homes in sports, and it's up to each of us to record the final hit that drives home the movement-defining run.

# John Amaechi and Tim Hardaway's "Tipping Point" Moment

***The day Matthew Shepard was killed***, America changed forever.

For decades people had been justified in—even encouraged by—viewing gay people as less than human. They were disgusting "perverts" whose "lifestyle" led to disease and (literally, according to many devout Christians) destruction. They couldn't reproduce, they were obsessed with sex, they couldn't remain monogamous (any more than straight people, anyway), and they hated the all-powerful American institution of sports. They weren't deserving of equality, and if an employer wanted to fire a gay person, more power to 'em.

On October 6, 1998, that was our country's collective mentality.

The next day two men kidnapped and beat twenty-one-year-old Matthew Shepard in Wyoming. They took him to a secluded field and, bloodied, tied him to a fence to die. He never saw another sunrise.

That was the day the homophobes lost the culture war.

It's easy to sit behind a keyboard and bang out anti-gay epithets. It's easy to carry years-held beliefs that gay people are deranged. It's easy to read the Bible, point to a select few passages in the 600-page book, and think homosexuality is an "abomination."

But when your mind is filled with images of an innocent

boy, sweet and fragile and blond, bloodied and bruised and tied to a fence left to freeze to death all because he's gay, the mind starts to rethink a lot of the shit that led to that point. When you look at the Pew Research Center's statistics, support for same-sex marriage jumped eight points from 1996 to 2001. It's no coincidence that it was after the brutal and much-publicized murder of Matthew Shepard. His death became the "tipping point" for gay rights in this country.

It's not as though John Amaechi was murdered nine years later. He wasn't. Not even close. It's almost disingenuous to mention the two incidents in the same chapter of a book. Yet the two moments as "tipping points" in our fight for LGBT equality are both incredibly important.

The former NBA journeyman for the Orlando Magic, the Utah Jazz, and a number of other teams came out publicly shortly after the Super Bowl in 2007. Amaechi was the first former NBA player, even the first former NCAA Division I basketball player, to come out publicly, sharing his news with *Outsports*, *ESPN*, and the Associated Press before the release of his tell-all book, *Man in the Middle*.

While we had seen a select few gay male former pro athletes come out publicly—Dave Kopay, Billy Bean, Esera Tuaolo—this was the first time current pro athletes were widely asked their opinion about the topic. In 2007, mainstream sports reporters who were afraid of getting punched in the face by one of their sports heroes if they posed a question about gay issues had the news "hook" to dip their toe in the waters.

The biggest names in the sport weighed in.

"Anybody who knows me knows I'm a guy who loves his teammates, and if anything ever comes up like that, I don't look at that," Miami Heat guard Dwyane Wade said. "I look at what guys can do for you on the court. And in the locker room you have great relationships with guys. I don't have any negative views."

Then–Boston Celtics coach Doc Rivers, who had coached Amaechi in Orlando: "[He's] better than a good kid; he's a fantastic kid. John Amaechi, when I was coaching him, was a great kid. He did as much charity work as anybody in our city, and he's still doing it. That's what I wish we focused on. Unfortunately, we're talking about his sexual orientation, which I couldn't care a flying flip about."

Isiah Thomas, then the coach of the New York Knicks: "If [there is an openly gay player] in my locker room, we won't have a problem with it. I can't speak for somebody else's locker room, but if it's in mine, we won't have a problem. I'll make damn sure there's no problem."

NBA commissioner David Stern: "We have a very diverse league. The question at the NBA is always, *Have you got game?* That's it, end of inquiry."

Players, coaches, league officials. For the first time reporters were asking people in pro sports the tough questions about a "gay topic" that had exploded into the headlines. And for the most part, they were incredibly positive.

In 2007, the outward support from the sports world was shocking. The assumption then—nine years after Shepard's death—had been that the sports world was not only desperately homophobic, but permanently so. The institution of sports was "the last closet." The military, where serving openly was illegal for gay soldiers, was viewed by some as more LGBT-friendly than sports. While it might seem mundane today that a commissioner of one of the Big Five sports leagues in America would vocalize support for a gay athlete, it would be years before a second commissioner did just that.

That made Tim Hardaway's comments stand out all the more.

A week after Amaechi's public revelation—Valentine's Day,

to be exact—Hardaway appeared on Dan Le Batard's Miami radio show talking basketball. The NBA All-Star Game—the game Hardaway had participated in five times as a member of the Golden State Warriors and Miami Heat—was around the corner. Le Batard asked Hardaway what he thought of Amaechi's public announcement. His answer—in February 2007—was something out of 1997.

"You know, I hate gay people, so I let it be known. I don't like gay people and I don't like to be around gay people. I am homophobic. I don't like it. It shouldn't be in the world or in the United States."

Hardaway didn't stop there. He specifically talked about having a gay teammate, and it got so much worse.

"And second of all, if he was on my team, I would, you know, really distance myself from him because, uh, I don't think that's right. And, you know, I don't think he should be in the locker room while we're in the locker room. I wouldn't even be a part of that."

That was the day the homophobes lost the culture war in *sports*.

"Hate" is a misunderstood word. So many of us toss it around like it's a Frisbee that it has lost a lot of its power. Usually.

New York Jets fans will talk about how they "hate" the New England Patriots. What they really mean is that the Patriots have kicked their ass for most of the last fifteen years and it drives them crazy. When the Jets beat the Patriots in the playoffs, do Gang Green fans really "hate" the team they just beat? No, they're just annoyed with the long-term success of the man in the gray hoodie.

A number of gay people have deemed every statement that doesn't support LGBT rights as "hate speech." Author Joe Wenke even went so far on the *Huffington Post* as saying that terms like "family" and "traditional family values" are forms of hate speech against gay people. I wish I could say he was simply being hyperbolic, but he meant it.

While many forms of distasteful expression roll off our tongues with ease in 2015, most Americans have no time for real hate.

Hardaway's comment—"I hate gay people"—was a wake-up call for many in sports. Athletes could say they don't understand being gay. Some might share discomfort with the idea of being naked next to a man who might want to be more than naked with him. New York Giants tight end Jeremy Shockey had told Howard Stern in 2002 that he didn't want to shower with a gay teammate. "That's not gonna work," he said at the time. Shockey felt some public blowback from it, but he had stopped short of where Hardaway ended up.

Hate?

"I hate gay people"?

It was a far less costly version of Shepard's ill-fated kidnapping. And, while no one died this time, the malice was still palpable in Hardaway's voice and words. When people heard it repeated on ESPN and on radio shows across the country for days, it gave pause to many.

*I might not accept gay people*, athletes told themselves, *but I don't hate them.* Hardaway had inferred that gay people shouldn't be allowed in pro sports because of how uncomfortable it made him.

*Keep gay people from sports? From jobs? No, man. That's not cool.*

The sports world came down on Hardaway in a very public way. It was like nothing we had seen since the career of sportscaster Jimmy "The Greek" Snyder was destroyed over racially insensitive comments.

Sacramento Kings owner Gavin Maloof weighed in on

Hardaway: "What he said was wrong. I'm sure he apologized for it, but the damage has been done. He should have never said that."

Former NBA point guard Steve Nash was diplomatic: "I don't think you'd catch many guys feeling that way . . . Maybe ten years ago. But in our locker room [now]? I think guys are over it."

Bill Laimbeer was typical Bill Laimbeer: "Who is Tim Hardaway? Next question."

Pat Riley, the coach of the Heat who had once coached Hardaway, said Hardaway's attitude "would not be tolerated in our organization."

When Hardaway refused to apologize later that day (though, after much pressure, he finally did), the overwhelming reaction spread far beyond quotes in a newspaper. Twenty-four hours after his comments, the Continental Basketball Association fired Hardaway from his role with a group bringing a new CBA team to Miami.

"The CBA does not in any way condone or endorse the hateful comments made by Mr. Hardaway to ESPN yesterday," said Dennis Truax, director of basketball operations for the CBA. "Mr. Hardaway's comments were unfortunate, hateful, and are not the views of the CBA or any of its member teams."

Mind you, this wasn't the well-established, multibillion-dollar NBA taking immediate action. This was the CBA, trying to do anything to bring attention to its league, firing a Miami sports legend with local cache the day after he made ninety seconds of comments about gay people.

The NBA followed suit. The league, which had invited Hardaway to be part of its upcoming All-Star Weekend festivities, told him not to show up. David Stern, the man who days earlier had expressed support for Amaechi and gay athletes, may have had the clearest and most damning reaction.

"We removed him from representing us because we didn't

think his comments were consistent with having anything to do with us," Stern said.

*Anything to do with us.*

*Anything.*

Leagues had taken action against players for anti-gay language in the past. The NFL once fined Steelers linebacker Joey Porter ten thousand dollars for calling Kellen Winslow a "fag." Major League Baseball suspended John Rocker for a few games after the Braves pitcher made comments to *Sports Illustrated* that were racist, homophobic, and, well, anti-everybody.

But the action taken by the NBA was a defining moment. It wasn't a fine, it wasn't a suspension. It was a complete rejection. The NBA—one of the Big Five sports leagues in America—was now on record: they were going to have absolutely nothing to do with homophobia.

Hardaway was even forced to remove his name from a car wash he owns in South Florida. *Tim Hardaway Presents Finest Hand Carwash* became *Grand Luxe Auto Bathe.*

The former Heat star was decimated by his own anti-gay words.

Within one week the sports world had seen its "tipping point" on gay issues. On February 7 it had collectively embraced a gay athlete, John Amaechi. The media had praised him for his courage. League leaders, team owners, coaches, players, and fans had wrapped their collective arms around him and thanked him for being true to himself.

A week later, those same people had completely and resoundingly rejected a homophobic athlete.

What's more, Hardaway was a far better NBA player than Amaechi. Hardaway was a first-round draft pick; Amaechi wasn't selected. Hardaway was a five-time All-Star; Amaechi was never considered.

In a sports world where performance on the court, ice, and field mean everything, the athlete who had proven himself over and over again was being rejected to support a little-name journeyman. In 2007 Amaechi was most famous for having come out publicly. Despite his incredible career—one that could in some circles be considered for the Hall of Fame—Hardaway became best known for being homophobic.

Amaechi's response to Hardaway was predictably brilliant and touched a larger issue at hand that Amaechi has made his calling card: pointing out hypocrisy. "It's not my place to get in the way of someone's relationship with God, with their God. That is their belief. However, if what you are actually talking about is biblical literalism, and if that's the case, then I expect people who spout vitriol about gay people to have the same ire as they regard players who have guns under their seats, who smoke marijuana, who commit adultery . . ."

There's an old saying about giving someone enough rope to hang themselves. That's long been Amaechi's tactic. While he's incredibly well-spoken and outspoken on a long list of social justice issues, he has used the very words of the bullies and haters to spell their own doom.

After every storm there is an opportunity for growth. Once the rain clouds pass and the sun peeks out, life has the opportunity to flourish.

Hardaway was pressured to eventually apologize publicly for his comments after initially declining. Most apologies of this sort essentially reflect a regret for being caught. *I'm sorry if anyone was offended* is the usual platitude. Translation: *I'm sorry you're too sensitive, but since I got caught, stay out of my business.*

Hardaway's regret ran deeper, and he expressed it publicly

without qualification. "I am committed to examining my feelings and will recognize, appreciate, and respect the differences among people in our society," he said. "I regret any embarrassment I have caused the league on the eve of one of their greatest annual events."

That first part—a commitment to examining how he thinks—was critical and something we had rarely seen. Only once before—when San Francisco 49ers running back Garrison Hearst apologized for saying he didn't want any "faggots" on his team— had we witnessed what appeared to be true contrition for anti-gay comments by a pro athlete. Yet even though Hearst's apology was complete and without reservation, it was also without clear next steps.

Soon after the incident, Hardaway disappeared. There was no basketball to pursue, no interviews to be done, no relationships with the CBA or NBA to develop. He became persona non grata. So he went to work. Quietly, behind the scenes, and without fanfare, Hardaway fulfilled his promise.

He engaged with organizations to learn more about the struggles of LGBT people, particularly kids. He took classes at the YES Institute in South Florida, whose mission is to "prevent suicide and ensure the healthy development of all youth through powerful communication and education on gender and orientation." He also worked with the Trevor Project, a group that runs a suicide hotline for LGBT teens. Through the two organizations Hardaway met some of the youth most affected by his comments, the very kids he was saying didn't belong in the locker room with him. As he met more gay people, his eyes opened to the destructive power of his words.

"With what I said, people could think it's okay to throw rocks at them or bully them," Hardaway eventually told Monte Poole of the Bay Area News Group in one of his first interviews, years after his infamous radio appearance. "I just wanted to make people understand that what I said wasn't cool. I wanted to make amends for it."

He went beyond an interview of contrition. Six years later, when Jason Collins became the first active player in the Big Five sports leagues to come out as gay, Hardaway offered proactive, vocal support. "I'm happy for him," Hardaway told the *Palm Beach Post*. "He is who he is and everybody's got to accept him for who he is."

When a push by religious conservatives was underway in El Paso to recall three elected officials who had voted to restore benefits for the partners of gay city employees, Hardaway—who had played basketball at the University of Texas at El Paso in the late eighties—fought against the recall. "I would say grow up and catch up with the times," he said. "It's all around the world . . . It's not right to not let the gays and lesbians have equal rights here."

In June 2013, petitioners leading the way toward same-sex marriage rights in Florida asked Hardaway to be the first person to sign their petition to put an equal marriage constitutional amendment on the Florida ballot. He signed the petition and spoke about the importance of bringing marriage equality to the state. "If you're married you're married—you should see your significant other in the hospital, make choices for your significant other if you need to make those choices."

All of this from a man who a few years earlier said, "I hate gay people," and became the face of homophobia in sports. Like the sports world as a whole, Hardaway has transformed into a model of inclusion.

Hardaway's long-term response to the controversy became a blueprint for athletes who let their ignorance get the best of them. While the pat "I apologize if you were offended" disclaimer is still

in play today, others learned from Hardaway and went further.
Many of them had gay friends or relatives, or their wives had gay
friends or relatives. Many of these athletes who'd hit the wrong
chord wanted to make amends. It showed.

While there were various incidents involving pro athletes' dumb comments about gay people in the years following
Hardaway's admission, none fell more clearly in the crosshairs
than those of San Francisco 49ers cornerback Chris Culliver. Just
days before the 49ers played the Baltimore Ravens in Super Bowl
XLVII in 2013, comedian Artie Lange asked Culliver about having a gay teammate in the wake of former 49er Kwame Harris's
arrest for allegedly beating his boyfriend.

"I don't do the gay guys. I don't do that," Culliver told Lange.
"We don't have any gay guys on the team. They gotta get up outta
here if they do. Can't be with that sweet stuff."

Never mind the bizarre "sweet stuff" comment, Culliver instantly became one of the biggest player-generated "distractions"
in the history of the Super Bowl as media descended on him and
the team for what was—just two months before Collins would
come out—a shocking admission of bigotry.

In his perfunctory apology, Culliver promised "to learn and
grow from this experience." He made good on his promise,
working with the Trevor Project to educate himself.

When the New York Giants hired David Tyree as a director
of player development, they inherited a potential public relations
nightmare due to the man's previous proactive battle against marriage equality. He had been one of the faces of the efforts by anti-gay
Christian groups to defeat same-sex marriage legislation in New
York in 2011. They lost.

Tyree and the Giants reached out to former NFL prospect
Wade Davis, who came out publicly in 2012, and myself to learn
more about gay issues. While it never involved an apology, the

intent to build bridges and find common ground was right out of Hardaway's playbook.

After calling NBA referee Bennie Adams a "faggot" during a 2011 regular season game, Kobe Bryant initially refused to apologize . . . then apologized . . . then committed to doing something to showcase his acceptance of LGBT people. He put his actions behind his words, recording an anti-homophobia public service announcement, appearing in YouTube's 2014 Pride video, and imploring a Twitter follower not to use anti-gay language.

This is what made Rajon Rondo's December 2015 episode, calling gay NBA referee Bill Kennedy a "faggot" during a game, so terrible. Not only did he and the NBA fail to acknowledge the incident until almost two weeks later, but Rondo's initial response over Twitter was eerily similar to the statement Bryant issued back in 2011, before eventually offering a true apology.Rondo served his one-game suspension and moved on, his reputation more deeply tarnished than it already had been.

When it comes to an apology, actions like those Bryant eventually took make amends a lot more powerfully than words.

There was one comment about the whole Hardaway situation that didn't get a lot of attention at the time, but which might have been the most ironically foretelling.

David Stern has been a big advocate of LGBT rights for years. A longtime supporter of left-wing Democratic politics, Stern set out years ago to open the league for gay players. When Phoenix Suns president Rick Welts came out publicly in 2011, Stern embraced his former league-office rising star.

Yet like Barack Obama, Hillary Clinton, and so many other Democrats, Stern played politics publicly with gay issues while privately supporting them. It was easy to take a strong stand when an ex-player said, "I hate gay people." But to really engage publicly in the conversation he would have to get ahead of America on the issue of LGBT equality. Stern wasn't ready to do that when Hardaway made his comments.

The Big Five sports leagues have long wanted to stay out of politics and groundbreaking social issues. Unless it's something easy like the NFL's embrace of the United Way or MLB's inner-city programs, they don't want to be embroiled in anything controversial. Reading the tea leaves and telling a homophobe not to show up for your all-star game is easy. But getting ahead of your fanbase and actively supporting same-sex marriage? Not even NFL commissioner Roger Goodell, whose brother is gay, would do that.

"This is an issue overall that has fascinated America," Stern said in refusing to make further comment about gay athletes in 2007, when most of the country opposed same-sex marriage. Then the whammy: "It's not an NBA issue."

Six years later, Jason Collins showed just how wrong Stern would be.

## Young Athletes Are Why There Will Never Be a "Gay Jackie Robinson"

*Before Michael Sam played* under any Friday night lights, before Robbie Rogers scored a single goal for the US Men's National Team, before Jason Collins blocked a shot for the New Jersey Nets, two young men in small-town football laid some of the first bricks on the path that led to these three men coming out publicly over a decade later.

When the story of Corey Johnson first crept into the public conscience in early 2000, some things made his story particularly surprising.

Johnson was the captain of his Masconomet High School football team in Topsfield, Massachusetts, about twenty miles north of Boston. Months earlier he had come out to his team as gay, a shocking revelation for a hard-hitting linebacker who had been elected captain of the team not long before. The public had heard of a couple gay football players—former pros Dave Kopay and Roy Simmons—but mostly they were anomalies, men who came out after their careers because, of course, you couldn't be gay and a football player at the same time. It wasn't possible. It wasn't allowed.

Johnson represented a shift in public consciousness. He was a football player. He was the captain of his football team. His football team was good. He was good. And he was gay. There were no gay football players on television at the time, none gracing the cover of *Sports Illustrated* or kissing their boyfriends on ESPN.

The most prominent gay character in the media at the time was Jack on *Will & Grace*—an over-the-top caricature of a gay man, the love child of Richard Simmons and Pee-Wee Herman.

Johnson was real—an all-American kid with a great smile and a big personality who could hit like a Mack Truck. He was instantly likable. His existence was shocking.

More shocking—and what the public hadn't ever seen before— was that Johnson's team embraced him. Gay sports leagues were popping up all around the world because mainstream high school, college, and weekend-warrior sports were simply not safe places for out LGBT people to participate. These all-gay leagues had to exist because straight teammates would reject you, and coaches would limit your playing time or simply kick you off the team. Parents would refuse to allow their sons or daughters to shower with you. That was the belief gay athletes—and many people in the general public—held in the late nineties: sports, and particularly team sports, were not a place for gay people.

That's the truth Johnson carried with him until he shared his secret with his team—and found the real truth. To be sure, women were already coming out in pro sports. Tennis greats Billie Jean King and Martina Navratilova had been open about their sexual orientations for two decades. The gay men in pro sports were still controversially silent.

When Johnson first came out to a teammate, a senior right tackle, the teammate cried. The tears weren't for having a gay person on the team, but rather because Johnson had felt the need to keep the secret to himself for so long. The empathy for Johnson's struggle drove his teammate to an emotional breakdown. It over-rode any fear he could have about Johnson seeing him naked in the locker room. Concern over what others might think was the farthest thing from his mind. In that moment, the straight teammate was moved by the truth that set Johnson free.

That was 1999. Tom Brady was in college. The Red Sox hadn't won the World Series in eight decades. Massachusetts wouldn't have gay marriage for four years.

When he told the rest of the team, word spread quickly. There was support, but it was tempered with trepidation and fear. *Football fag* showed up on a wall at the school. Some of the team feared they would be labeled gay because their cocaptain was a homo. It was uncharted territory for everyone. No other student—athlete or not—was openly gay at the school of 1,200 kids. There were no publicly out active football players at any level in the world.

When someone asked to revote on the captainship of the team given Johnson's revelation, the head coach stepped in. "We simply said this is not open for discussion," coach Jim Pugh told ESPN at the time. "The whole idea of stripping his captaincy is more divisive than Corey coming out could ever be."

The team's initial fears of the unknown quickly dissipated, replaced by hard-fought practices and games. Johnson was one of the leaders of the team, personable, popular, and aggressive on the field. By October the team was found serenading him with the Village People's uber-gay classic "Y.M.C.A." on the bus ride home from an away game. Concerns about their gay teammate's sexual orientation were gone. The occasional opposing player made a homophobic crack, but it was usually the Masconomet team coming out on top. When you win lots of football games, you don't really care very much if the other team takes a jab about a gay teammate.

Johnson had learned the truth about sports: there might be some initial trepidation with having a gay teammate, but it goes away quickly when everybody starts hitting each other.

The following year and a few hundred miles away, a gay student at Bloomsburg University in central Pennsylvania also severely underestimated the power of the bonds of a football team.

Recently broken up from the football team's deeply closeted captain—Brian Sims—that jilted student told one of the other football players that their captain was gay, with the hope that the team would kick Sims to the curb. Revealing his secret to his homophobic teammates would be the ultimate revenge for their ended relationship. Or so he thought.

Late one night the teammate in the know asked Sims if he was gay. It all added up for the teammate: Sims was handsome, popular, and the captain of the football team, yet when cute co-eds found their way into Sims's room late at night they were always sent packing within a matter of minutes.

"I feared it would change the dynamic in the locker room," Sims said about his initial decision not to come out to his team. "You're spending four or five hours a day with your friends, and that's what I played for. I cared that my team would still be comfortable around me."

Despite the fear, Sims answered his teammate's question honestly; he was gay. They spent much of the rest of the night talking about the revelation, mostly making sure that Sims was in good shape emotionally. The teammate was confident the guys on the team would handle it well. Word spread to their teammates slowly. This was before MySpace and Facebook; in 2000, no one was tweeting about anyone's sexual orientation. The guys Sims soon told didn't hold a team meeting, but slowly more and more teammates found out.

It shocked most of the team. Just like Johnson, Sims didn't fit the mold that most of the guys on the team had for gay men. In his senior year he was 6' tall, 260 pounds, and bench-pressed 225 pounds thirty-seven times. He was a "guy's guy": no limp wrist, no feather boas.

While Sims didn't share his story publicly until years later, Johnson became an immediate media sensation in 2000, a gay-football unicorn if we had ever seen one. The venerable Bob Lipsyte wrote a lengthy page A1 feature piece for the *New York Times*. *20/20* did a segment on Johnson and his team. Johnson spoke at the Millennium March on Washington advocating for equality for gay Americans.

Yet even separated by a number of years, the reaction to the two stories was almost identical. People were inspired and educated. Stereotypical attitudes about gay people were challenged, the perception of straight football players as knuckle-dragging homophobes turned upside down.

Something maybe even more important happened for both of these young men. At the end of their stories on *Outsports*, we included their e-mail addresses. Out gay athletes were few and far between, and these two guys wanted to hear from people who might need some help and guidance, or just someone to listen. In the first year, Johnson received over a thousand e-mails. He still gets e-mails today from that story, seventeen years later. Sims had to take off several days from work at his law firm just to answer the hundreds of e-mails he received.

Gay athletes—and specifically gay football players—suddenly had people like them with whom to connect. Two key dominoes had been knocked over.

For years people have asked me about when we would see the "gay Jackie Robinson." There are two ways to look at that: 1) we already have, and 2) we never will.

When Jackie Robinson broke the color barrier in Major League Baseball, it was at a time when racism was a dominant force in every corner of society. The Ku Klux Klan plagued the South. Segregation was alive and well from Boston to Kansas City. African Americans were barred from voting, they were banned from equal education, and they were denied many employment opportunities. Interracial marriage was illegal in most states.

In 1947, Robinson was a harbinger of change to come. He experienced threats and needed special protection to keep him safe on road trips. Players refused to compete against him. Yet there he was, every day from April to September, swinging a bat and rounding the bases. His participation in sports advanced the cause.

The time for a singular LGBT athlete to step into that role has come and gone. Certainly all is not perfect for LGBT people in America. While many see the fight for marriage equality in the rearview mirror, many politicians—mostly Republicans—still aim to strip gay and trans people and same-sex couples of their rights. It is still legal in twenty-nine states—the majority of America—to fire someone for being gay, as sexual orientation has not been granted federal civil rights protection.

Yet the day when an athlete can be ahead of the curve on LGBT human-rights issues in America has passed. Gay people can vote. Gay people aren't relegated to a particular seat on a bus. Out gay people have been playing sports with straight people for years. Is it perfect? No. Trans people in particular still face major issues in public accommodations and sports participation. Yet the state of LGBT rights in 2016 simply isn't in the same century as the civil rights of African Americans in 1947.

Instead, the closest thing we've had to a "gay Jackie Robinson" were people like Johnson, Sims, and other LGBT athletes and coaches at the high school and college level who came out publicly and to their teams in the eighties, nineties, and early 2000s. These people, in the trenches of small-town communities and lower-profile teams, collectively helped pave the way not just for future gay athletes, but their public profiles—both locally and nationally—shifted the conversation and bolstered legal advancements including marriage equality.

If there has ever been one "seminal" LGBT sports figure, it is Dave Kopay. While he had already retired when he came out in 1975, he was years ahead of Billie Jean King and Martina Navratilova. And while both women were pushed out of the closet—King by a lawsuit, and Navratilova by a newspaper article—Kopay decided to take the step all on his own because it was the right thing to do.

Andrew Goldstein as well stands out as singular, though much less well-known. The lacrosse goalie came out publicly in 2005 while at Dartmouth and was the first out gay man drafted by a pro sports league when the Boston Cannons selected him in the Major League Lacrosse draft later that year. Yet it's impossible to assign him "Jackie Robinson" status given his short two-year stay in lacrosse and the much lower profile of the sport.

Bill Tilden is arguably the greatest male tennis player of all time, winning ten Grand Slams in the 1920s, at a time when he only had access to one or two a year. From 1918 to 1930 he advanced to at least the semifinals of all but one Grand Slam tournament he entered. While he was known in tennis circles to be gay, he didn't publicly acknowledge it until he was arrested for soliciting a minor; he went on to distance himself from his homosexuality, calling it an "illness" for which he was being treated. Hardly the actions of a "gay Jackie Robinson."

People say Collins and Rogers and Sam changed the conversation and helped bring change. And they did, to an extent. But their coming-out stories were more the result of the conversation already having changed, thanks to the aforementioned athletes, along with others. They didn't start or end the conversation, though they were three more (very big) dominoes.

Truth be told, all social-justice movements are bottom-up. It took hundreds of local politicians and a number of states to legalize same-sex marriage before President Obama would admit that he did, in fact, support it too. Social justice in sports hasn't been any different.

Before Jackie Robinson played for the Brooklyn Dodgers, there was Kenny Washington. Washington was a standout running back for UCLA who had attracted the interest of Chicago Bears coach George Halas in 1940. Until that time, the NFL was lily white, from the towel boys to the players to the coaches. Halas was blocked by the other NFL owners from signing Washington to a contract. Six years later, Washington was signed by and suited up for his hometown Los Angeles Rams. In 1946, a year before Jackie Robinson broke through, the NFL had seen its first black player take the field.

Yet to understand just how backward professional sports leagues are on social issues, you need only look at William H. Lewis. He was one of the very first black college football players, taking the field for Amherst College in 1888. Two years later, the mostly white Amherst players elected Lewis their team captain. After graduating from Amherst, he went to Harvard, where he played football for the Crimson and eventually spent twelve seasons as a coach. All of this was almost sixty years before Washington integrated the NFL, and ninety years before the NFL would have its first African American head coach.

I do have to offer this asterisk. In 1920, a black football player out of Brown University named Fritz Pollard played for—and the following year coached—the Akron Pros. It was the nascent years of the NFL when a team's running back could also be its coach. By 1926 Pollard and the handful of black players in the NFL were all removed from the league, never to be seen in an NFL uniform again. So while Pollard does have some historic distinction, it's hard to say he integrated the sport given no blacks were allowed for two decades after he left.

Despite William H. Lewis breaking the color barrier for

players and coaches in college football, over a century later his name has been forgotten. Chances are slim to none you've seen this man's name before reading it here. We as a society give little credence to the incredible advancements made every day in high school and college athletics, focusing our key societal milestones on the pros.

It's the same dynamic with gay athletes. A hundred years from now people won't remember Corey Johnson or Brian Sims for being gay athletes. Guys like Conner Mertens and Mitch Eby—the first two college football players to come out to the media while still playing—will be long forgotten.

But we'll remember Michael Sam. We'll remember Jason Collins. Robbie Rogers won't be forgotten. The contribution these men have made by coming out while they were still playing—and in Sam's case before his professional career even started—is strong, and their statuses as visible role models are profound, no doubt. That's their most impactful contribution. Yet they came out after their leagues had already changed policy on sexual orientation, and they followed countless others who had come out in sports at the lower levels. None are the "gay Jackie Robinson." That's not to diminish their courage or personal journey; yet we can't overstate the importance of those younger kids at the lower levels of sports who helped pave the way for them.

It's easy to understand our collective dismissal of groundbreaking high school and college athletes and the over-elevation of elite athletes. Professional athletes are on the covers of magazines. They're on television every day. They are, frankly, better athletes, and a culture that embraces the best will . . . embrace the best. Jackie Robinson playing professional baseball gave him a much bigger national platform than playing for UCLA, which in the 1940s was of only regional interest. Robinson was also a better athlete than Washington—which is why one has Hollywood movies made about him and the other is forgotten.

Yet there's another dynamic that plays into the over-the-moon praising of pro gay athletes and the deflation of the social-justice accomplishments of those in high school and college: risk.

You can't become a hero in our culture without risking something. When Pete Carroll allowed a pass play to be called at the end of Super Bowl XLIX, he knew that if it worked he would be lauded as a genius with balls of steel. Sure, he could have run the ball in with Marshawn Lynch, but putting the ball in the air? When everyone knows there are three possible outcomes to a pass play and two are bad? To toss immortality into the air and hope it lands in the right hands, with the best short-yardage running back in the league and possibly one of the best running quarterbacks of all time? If that play had worked, with that risk involved, he would have gone from "elite coach" to "immortal coach."

It didn't work out for him.

Yet it's that same dynamic for gay athletes coming out.

When Corey Johnson came out to his football team, the worst thing that could have happened would have been getting cut from the team before his senior season in high school. It would have been sad, it would have been potentially harmful to his psyche, but he wouldn't have lost his job or any future he possibly had in sports. He didn't play football in college—he didn't attend college. While his two Gay Super Bowl championships in 2006 and 2007 with me on the New York Warriors flag football team are lovely, they didn't help him get where he is today.

When Jason Collins came out, in the eyes of the media and the public, he was risking the rest of his career. He was risking his endorsement deal with Nike. He risked his entire NBA legacy.

When Robbie Rogers came out, he was risking his bright future in soccer so much that he felt the need to quit the game in the same breath he told us he was gay.

When Michael Sam came out, he risked his entire professional career.

While high school and college athletes certainly put their friendships on the line, they don't risk much financially by coming out. These pro athletes? The perception is that they risk it all. That risk makes them heroes.

This is also one of the reasons women coming out are treated differently: there is simply a different perceived risk. While women have been fired from coaching jobs and kicked off college teams for being gay, the assumption by the public is that there is no homophobia in women's sports, none of them have big endorsement deals, and there is no real risk of losing anything by coming out. It's not remotely true, but those are the assumptions. Female athletes are also largely not put by our society in the same pantheon as NFL and NBA players—it is unfortunate, but it's also reality.

Despite the values our society puts on the careers of athletes, risk is relative. Me putting a thousand dollars on red-19 is a much bigger risk than Kobe Bryant making the same bet. Even in the worst-case scenario, a gay professional athlete coming out publicly and losing a million dollars in salary and endorsement deals can be a lot less costly than a teenage soccer player coming out in Wichita, losing her friends, and being kicked out of her home by her parents.

The risk young people take by coming out of the closet in their personal lives, and then publicly, is profound. The public, addicted to the faces on television, red carpets, and green money, simply doesn't see it that way.

Yet each one of those young people is the closest thing to a "gay Jackie Robinson" we'll ever get.

\* \* \*

One element of risk for professional athletes has been completely overblown: the loss of endorsement deals.

No doubt athletes in the past have lost access to those sweet contracts. Martina Navratilova estimates she lost millions in endorsement deals in the 1980s because she came out publicly. She's probably right.

Today, however, that risk is arguably nonexistent. Major corporations like Nike, Visa, and Marriott have embraced out athletes like Brittney Griner, Jason Collins, and Michael Sam. When Adidas announced in 2016 that it would not drop an endorsed athlete because she or he came out, the response was little more than shrugs: they were stating the obvious.

After Sam came out publicly in 2014, some people speculated that he did it to bring in endorsement deals, and criticism was levied that he received too many opportunities to make money outside of his sport.

For those who take the risk at any level, the rewards can in fact be tremendous.

Corey Johnson moved to San Francisco after high school, then to New York City where he made his home. He worked as an activist at GLAAD—the country's largest LGBT media watchdog. He also worked in real estate, and he even had a radio show in the nascent days of Sirius Radio.

Johnson's story "ends" fifteen years later in incredible triumph. In 2013 he was elected to the New York city council, replacing Christine Quinn as she aimed to become the first out gay person elected mayor of New York City. His high school football story of over fifteen years ago is still significant, as ESPN aired a feature piece on him and his team shortly after Michael Sam came out.

Brian Sims has also parlayed his leadership into a political career. In 2012 he became the first openly gay person ever elected to the Pennsylvania House of Representatives. He won reelection in 2014, running unopposed.

Both of these men have made advancing LGBT issues a priority in their political careers. For Johnson in New York City, that hasn't been hard. A poll of New York State residents in 2014 found that 65 percent of them supported same-sex marriage rights. And that's including Western New York, which is essentially a "red" state. In New York City, with Democrats holding 94 percent of the city council seats, LGBT issues are easily supported.

Sims has faced other challenges. Pennsylvania is the epitome of a "purple" state, and equality for LGBT people has not come easily. When a court legalized same-sex marriage in May 2014, less than half of Pennsylvania residents supported the ruling. Within six months of legalization, another poll found that almost two thirds—62 percent—supported it. It's hard to argue that Sims's many speeches about LGBT equality, and his stature as a successful college football captain in central Pennsylvania, didn't morph into a powerful force for equality.

What's clear from both of these men is the power of young LGBT athletes to lead outside the lines. For years, Corey Johnson has been mentioned as a potential future mayor of New York City. Sims's meteoric rise in Pennsylvania politics has him on a Washington, DC trajectory at the very highest levels, already declaring his candidacy for Congress in 2016. While these men may not have received the coast-to-coast, wall-to-wall media coverage with which Jason Collins and Michael Sam dominated entire news cycles, the work they have pursued after their high school and college sports careers ended have built legacies of equality that rival even the great Dave Kopay and Harvey Milk.

*Derrick Gordon and the Un-intended Consequence of the Locker Room's Casual Words*

***Derrick Gordon's legs literally shook*** as he stood in front of his University of Massachusetts teammates in early April 2014 preparing to share a secret. The shooting guard had had a successful season, starting every game for the team as a red-shirt sophomore and finishing fourth on the team in scoring. Yet buried beneath a mountain of fear had been the undeniable fact that he is gay. After years of looking over his shoulder, isolating himself from his teammates, and worrying if someone had somehow discovered his unforgivable secret, the power of his own truth had led him to the decision to reveal his true identity not just with his teammates and coaches, but with the world.

When Gordon stood before his team and told them he's gay, he shared with them his emotional struggle of the previous year. He choked up as he talked about being teased by the very teammates sitting before him. He shared the suffering of his inability to connect with all the locker-room talk about sex with women. He felt like an outsider, and that kept him from being the best teammate he could be.

Gordon, a macho kid from a rough-and-tumble neighborhood in New Jersey, cried in front of his teammates. Many of them teared up as well.

He had nearly quit the sport of basketball earlier that season. After sitting out the 2012–13 season (per NCAA rules) due to transferring from Western Kentucky University, Gordon found himself the butt of jokes and teasing from his teammates about being gay. He had only come to accept his sexual orientation in recent years—the "straight" front he felt he had to put up in public was at odds with who he really was.

The fact that Gordon is gay was something he kept from the team, but that shroud of secrecy didn't stop the other young men from pouncing on him from the beginning. The team had reason for suspicion after Gordon was tagged in an Instagram photo taken outside a New Jersey gay bar the previous summer. His UMass teammates would slip in snide comments on the court or give Gordon an anti-gay verbal smack jab in the locker room.

It was nothing any of them hadn't said or heard in high school. Whether it was their AAU coach launching a "sissy" their way after a failed dunk, or a teammate talking about the "faggots" they would crush on the court that night, using "gay" language to beat down other athletes had been inherent to their sports experience: playing sports and demeaning people with gay epithets went hand-in-hand. Boys will be boys.

Gordon denied being gay over and over after the teasing started—the Instagram photo, he said, was just an overeager fan who recognized Gordon as he walked past the random bar. It wasn't true, but it was Gordon's cover and he was sticking to it. Some of the team bought it—others weren't so sure. Either way, the jabbing didn't go away, it got worse.

The treatment from the team went beyond locker room banter. Most of the players began avoiding him in the showers. On the UMass men's basketball roster, there were only two white players: according to Gordon, an African American, they were the only teammates willing to shower with him. Every one of the other black players kept their towels around their waists until

Gordon was back at his locker getting dressed. With their words and subtle actions, the team was alienating him.

The athletes had no idea what they were doing and the effect it was having on their teammate.

It all took its toll. Before the 2013–14 basketball season started in November, Gordon considered quitting basketball altogether. While the sport had lifted him out of a broken-down neighborhood in New Jersey, the emotional pain was becoming too much for him to bear.

Gordon isolated himself from the rest of the team, staying alone in his room most nights. Sometimes he would venture to the solitude of the gym, with music pumping through his headphones. He put on twenty-five pounds of muscle in just a couple years. During the entire 2013–14 school year after the harassment started, Gordon never went to a single party on campus. His intense, fiery persona on court morphed into that of a quiet, meek hermit once the game was over. He had a secret he would guard until the coroner pried the basketball from his hands.

The homophobia he encountered in the locker room was driving him from the sport.

Casual words. That's all locker room homophobia is to the athletes and coaches who toss around "faggot," "sissy," and "dyke" as alleged motivational tools. By associating a missed shot or a dropped pass with being gay, lesbian, or even transgender, you make young athletes work harder. At least, that's what the old-school mentality espouses.

For many straight athletes, it hits the bull's-eye. While the dynamic is changing in our culture, the worst thing you can call many straight men is still "gay." Whether they admit it or not, most of them are deeply motivated by the avoidance of that label. Associating a missed tackle with that word? The straight athlete has added incentive to make the right play the next time around.

Yet for gay athletes like Gordon, that language isn't just an annoyance, it's a crushing blow.

For decades it was believed gay men simply didn't participate in sports outside of a few very rare exceptions who had somehow slipped through the cracks. There was no consideration for the mental well-being of gay people in the locker room, as they were presumed to be relegated to the cheerleading squad or the stands; those were the "sissies" none of the men of the gridiron wanted any part of. A language grew up around that assumption that made "fags" the "other" in the locker room, assuming none of them were there (and frankly, in the unenlightened culture of the sixties and seventies, the language likely would have persisted even with them there).

Like the opposing team, gay men were the enemy. The NFL head of security throughout the 1970s, Jack Danahy, even publicly doubted whether there was a single gay man in the NFL.

"If there were actually a homosexual in the league, which I have no evidence there is, if you have a homosexual, he's always subject to possible compromise," Danahy said. He claimed he had no evidence that there was a "homosexual" in the league despite David Kopay—an NFL running back for five teams over nine seasons—having just come out publicly and saying very clearly that he knew of others on his Redskins team.

Danahy's ensuing comments reveal just how deeply the NFL—and football in general—loathed the idea of gays on the team: "In espionage, there's been a history in international affairs of homosexuals being compromised and used against their better interests, so that would naturally be a matter of concern to us."

To the NFL head of security in the mid-seventies, gays weren't just unwanted in sports, they were a threat to the very security of what would in two decades become America's most popular sports league. Worrying about how a few of them might feel hearing the word "faggot" in the locker room?—it was as foreign of an idea as having a woman quarterback the New York Jets.

Out gay Major League Soccer player Robbie Rogers calls it a "pack mentality." When all the wolves are after the same thing (namely, athletic glory and hot women), anything goes. For those few people in the pack who might be after something else (namely, other men), that difference gets accentuated in their minds to sometimes an emotionally overwhelming boiling point.

For the pack to realize its true potential, it's up to the collective to adjust its behavior when one of the reindeer has a slightly different nose. If not, the potential stars who might be slightly different will go away—there will be no sleigh ride on a foggy Christmas Eve.

This belies the importance of sharing the stories of as many LGBT people in sports as possible. With the awareness that there could be a gay man in every locker room in America comes an increasing sensitivity to the need for consideration in every corner of sports.

For women it's a dynamic turned upside down. While many people in sports for decades doubted that any gay male athletes reached elite levels, the stereotypical assumption is that all women who play in the NCAA or WNBA are lesbians. That gets used as a weapon in a very different way.

Jourdan Sayers, the out soccer goalie for Columbia University, talked about hearing teammates call other teams "a bunch of dykes"—but only when Columbia lost a game. Demeaning the victors for their athletic prowess was a way of coping with loss, alienating them subconsciously in their minds.

"They were essentially saying, *They're only good because they're masculine,*" Sayers remembered, "*so they're not like us.*" Sayers never heard the Columbia team call themselves "dykes" when they beat another team.

None of Derrick Gordon's teammates had meant to push him to the brink of depression. They never do. Straight athletes use "faggot" and "sissy" and "that's so gay" as short-hand for "weak" and "you're not pulling your weight on the team."

The very reason "faggot" translates into "weak" in the minds of so many is because of the decades of portrayals of gay people as delicate pansies interested only in Broadway musicals and Judy Garland numbers. When a gay male character from *Will & Grace* dates someone who enjoys sports, he's portrayed as sports illiterate, needing to rely on a woman's expertise to show him the ropes. When *Modern Family*'s uber-gay Jesse Tyler Ferguson goes to a New York Knicks game, he has to play to stereotype, tweeting: *I'm excited to go to my first NBA "sports game" tonight with my fake boyfriend @ericstonestreet*, and, *Go Knicks! Throw the orange ball around!*

The conscious reason athletes employ this language usually isn't to chastise gay people, though Rajon Rondo directing the word at NBA referee Bill Kennedy in December 2015 certainly carried that intent. The slur is often meant simply to convey some form of displeasure. When Kobe Bryant called referee Bennie Adams a "fucking faggot" in a 2011 NBA game, he didn't mean that Adams was gay. Bryant was quick to say that of course he didn't mean anything anti-gay; he has gay friends and doesn't have a homophobic bone in his body (even though, subconsciously, he did). In the following days even Bryant came to realize the root meaning of the word and how, whether he meant it to be anti-gay or not, that's what it was.

"For me, it's about the bigger message," Bryant told ESPN in the days after he was fined $100,000 by the NBA for his slur. "I made a mistake in terms of what I said, but it's also the responsibility it carries with it. I don't want kids to think that it's okay or cool to call kids that or tease them because of that. I don't stand for that. I never have. I've been in so many altercations in middle school and in high school protecting kids from that. I certainly won't be part of enhancing that and the feeling that it's okay. I just won't."

While the straight athlete like Bryant using the language simply means, *You just fucked up*, the gay athlete on the receiving end hears, literally, *I hate you*.

In talking with so many LGBT athletes over the years, I've found this disconnect in language to be the most powerful force keeping athletes in the closet. When you think you hear, *I hate you*, on a daily basis, where is the space to open up and be honest with your team about who you are?

It wasn't just the explicit anti-gay language that pushed Gordon away from his team and into depression. The overt heterosexism of the daily conversations on the team had a powerful effect.

Imagine being in a locker room, all the guys in some state of undress, and one of your teammates starts talking about this "hot chick" he "banged" the night before. He starts describing her in detail, from the size of her chest to the curve of her ass. Sitting there on the bench overhearing the posturing, a gay athlete turns back to his locker, picks up his phone, and engages with the outside world, leaving behind his teammates standing next to him.

Another teammate pipes up that he knows that girl—"She's smokin' hot." They high-five. A third teammate joins in the conversation about his girlfriend. She was away at her parents' house for the weekend and she's back tonight. He's got an evening planned, an early dinner and a long session of sex that will consume the rest of the night. He's had trouble being loyal because there's this hot girl in English class giving him the eye. She even sexted him a couple of hot photos. The guys gather around his phone to check her out. Laughs, more high fives.

Sitting there, still unable to avoid the talk of his teammates bonding over their straightness, the gay athlete essentially has three options.

First, he could join in the conversation with honesty. *Yeah, I've been texting with this hot dude from the tennis team. Such a nice ass on him. Want to see pictures of his dick?* Insert proverbial record-scratch, jaws dropping, teammates walking away. Even if the reaction isn't that severe, there is a level of virtually guaranteed rejection for a gay athlete trying to share his own sexual conquests with his team. Even the coolest, most gay-friendly environment will devolve into some kind of light-hearted joking that helps the straight athletes show they're not down with gay sex. For guys like Gordon, deeply closeted and struggling with their own identities, the first option is a no-go.

The second choice is to fit in by lying. When speculation started about him being gay, Gordon brought one of his ex-girlfriends to campus to throw off the scent. He was used to it—he'd been lying about his sexual orientation his entire adult life. Truth is, most closeted LGBT athletes go this route, choosing to bury their true feelings and tell their teammates what they want to hear instead of what the gay athlete wants to tell them. They'll make sure to be seen leaving a party with the hottest girl in the room, or they'll even have sex—sometimes with a teammate within earshot—to prove they're anything but gay. While Gordon started down this path, it was one he couldn't bear.

The last option is to just stay silent, not say anything at all. Among closeted lives filled with struggle, this path of least resistance is the most popular choice. It's the path Gordon chose to walk with his UMass team. When teammates headed out to celebrate a big victory—and they started the 2013–14 season with eleven of them in a row—Gordon returned to his room by himself. When casual friends trudged through the snow to a party on a Friday night, he would turn away the invitation and visit the gym by himself. He ate meals alone. As the school year wore on, he cried himself to sleep, the isolation consuming his mental state.

"I just wanted to run and hide somewhere," Gordon told me days before he came out to his team and to the public. "Nobody should ever feel that way. I kept to myself a lot. Most of the time when you see me on campus, I'm alone. I didn't go to any parties at all. My day-to-day here, I do the same thing over and over every day . . . That was probably the lowest point I was at, because that was the time I didn't want to play basketball anymore."

The disconnection between what is said and what is heard is always made crystal clear when the athlete comes out. Virtually every single one of the athletes who has come out publicly in the last fifteen years says the same thing: Before they came out, they were full of torment driven largely by the homophobic comments they heard from their teammates and by the lack of connection they had to their straight sex–driven conversations. Then, once they were honest with the team, that anti-gay language went away, replaced by understanding and compassion.

When Gordon came out to his team, it took a toll on the very athletes who had nearly driven him from basketball. As he spoke, some of the guys who were the most vicious were moved emotionally by the struggle they had been subjecting Gordon to. There was hardly a dry eye in the room.

Many of those young men had never had someone close to them come out. It was unchartered territory for everyone in the room, including head coach Derek Kellogg. Gordon's move was unprecedented in sports: no Division I college basketball player had ever come out publicly. Heck, no one had done it in football, baseball, or hockey either.

It had taken Gordon four years from the first time he realized he might be gay to finally tell some of his teammates. So it shouldn't have come as a surprise when half of the players called another team meeting the following day. This time, they implored Gordon to stay quiet about his sexual orientation and not go to the media.

Oops. Gordon and the UMass athletic department had already mapped out a media strategy that included articles by Kate Fagan at *ESPN* and me at *Outsports*, plus a likely press conference the day the stories appeared. In fact, I had been talking with Gordon for two weeks, taking notes in the moments after he came out to his family and coach, as he met other gay people in sports like Wade Davis and high school basketball coach Anthony Nicodemo, and as he struggled with exactly how to tell his team. The proverbial ship had already sailed.

Yet the team wanted him to stay quiet.

In that moment, they felt the fear Gordon had lived with for years. The straight athletes themselves had bought into the idea that sports are a homophobic place where gay people weren't welcome. The subconscious became very conscious for them. They told Gordon they were suddenly concerned about having to talk to their friends, girlfriends, and family about having a gay teammate. They didn't have a problem with his sexual orientation, they simply didn't want it to define them or the team.

They now understood, at a deep level, what it was like to be "other" in a sports landscape designed for straight guys to strut their stuff. They were suddenly worried about being labeled "gay by association."

At the same time Gordon had been considering leaving his sport, offensive tackle Jonathan Martin quit the Miami Dolphins. Martin had been the quiet victim of prolonged harassment from at least three teammates in the months leading up to his departure from the team. While the perpetrators and other teammates discredited Martin publicly, Ted Wells—the lawyer hired by the National Football League to dig into the situation—made it abundantly clear that Martin had been the victim of his teammates' tormenting.

"The report concludes that three starters on the Dolphins offensive line—Richie Incognito, John Jerry, and Mike Pouncey—engaged in a pattern of harassment directed at not only Jonathan Martin, but also another young Dolphins offensive lineman and an assistant trainer," Wells declared with the release of the report. "The report finds that the assistant trainer repeatedly was the object of racial slurs and other racially derogatory language; that the other offensive lineman was subjected to homophobic name-calling and improper physical touching; and that Martin was taunted on a persistent basis with sexually explicit remarks about his sister and his mother and at times ridiculed with racial insults and other offensive comments."

Maybe the most insightful revelation Wells unearthed wasn't that Martin's accusations were true, but rather the nuance behind the motivations of his teammates: "The report concludes that the harassment by Martin's teammates was a contributing factor in his decision to leave the team, but also finds that Martin's teammates did not intend to drive Martin from the team or cause him lasting emotional injury."

Think about that disconnect. Martin was "taunted on a persistent basis with sexually explicit remarks about his sister and his mother and at times ridiculed with racial insults and other offensive comments," yet the people harassing him didn't intend to cause "lasting emotional injury."

Huh? If you mix together some butter, flour, and sugar, throw in some chocolate chips, and stick it in the oven, you intend to bake cookies. If you send a resignation letter to your boss, you intend to quit your job. Yet when you torment someone about his sexual orientation, race, and family, you don't intend to inflict harm?

This only makes sense to someone brainwashed by the "lore of the locker room."

The dynamic gets at the core traditional culture of male sports locker rooms. They're like fraternity houses. "Real men" are supposed to be desensitized to teasing. If you can't take some friendly banter from teammates about *yo' mama,* then how are you going to face down a 6'10" forward driving the basket? If you can't handle some jibing about your sexual orientation, how can your teammates expect you to block that linebacker looking to break your quarterback into tiny little pieces?

What these men don't see is that teasing and harassment do not lead to productivity. Period. Players on teams at the very top of the food chain taunt and name-call just as much as the cellar-dwellers. Would the teammates of Martin and Gordon argue that successful players on winning teams harass one another more effectively? That they're just better at getting under the skin of the guys on whom they rely for victory?

We're told daily that a gay athlete will only be measured by his ability to help a team win because that's all that matters. But when it comes to hazing, it's a different standard. Who could possibly argue that the taunting and harassment of athletes actually lead to more victories, when both successful and unsuccessful teams engage in hazing and other forms of alienating athletes in the name of "bonding"?

The pro sports leagues are claiming to take active roles in addressing this. At the NFL Annual Meeting in March 2014, St. Louis Rams coach Jeff Fisher, a member of the league's competition committee, said sportsmanship was a significant topic of conversation amongst owners, coaches, and front office executives. He said the NFL will double its efforts to address taunting not just on the field—where reported incidents had tripled over the previous year—but also in the locker room.

Sadly, some people across the NFL have shown they are not always serious about actually addressing the behavior. It's easy to make some grand pronouncements about it at a meeting, but when it comes time to pursue the action, sometimes the accusers and the people in power let it fade away.

When New York Giants wide receiver Odell Beckham Jr. claimed through several former players and his team that he was the target of homophobic slurs in a game against the Carolina Panthers, everyone involved quickly shut up about it. The league did a perfunctory look into the claim and found no concrete "evidence." The Giants never filed a complaint or spoke publicly about the incident. The Panthers denied Beckham was ever taunted, despite video of a Panthers player carrying around a baseball bat before the game and pursuing Beckham during warmups.

Beckham himself let the issue of homophobia drift away, failing to speak out publicly or raise the issue during the hearing on his one-game suspension for illegal hits.

It's those illegal hits, targeting Panthers cornerback Josh Norman after his alleged gay slurs toward Beckham, that demonstrate the true power of these words. Beckham and Norman were both punished for physical hits but no action was taken on the non-physical taunting. "Everybody get back to the game, nothing to see here."

The NBA, in addressing bullying, has also sent a memo to its teams making clear that taunting, teasing, and name-calling on the court and in any workplace—including the locker room—will not be tolerated.

A pro sports locker room is not a fraternity house, it's a workplace. Whether they're unionized, given scholarships, or paid out-right, the young men and women in high school and college athletics deserve the same environment free from harassment, from a small Division III school like Maine Maritime Academy all the way to big-time televised programs like Syracuse and the University of Florida.

The environment of pro sports locker rooms is already a lot better than the locker rooms at other levels. Michael Irvin told me that when he was in high school he heard anti-gay language like "faggot" all the time. In college at the University of Miami he heard it less, and he said he can't recall ever hearing that word in the Dallas Cowboys locker room of the 1990s.

Chris Kluwe, who sued the Minnesota Vikings over anti-gay harassment claiming he was released by the team for his support of same-sex marriage, said he only heard explicit anti-gay hatred in the Vikings locker room "once or twice" in his eight seasons there.

The diversity of our society today mandates a different handling of locker room culture. It's not political correctness, it's simply building an environment in which each athlete feels welcome and embraced. It's within that culture that an athlete can blossom. How does verbally berating athletes and throwing around anti-gay or racial slurs help an athlete feel at home? How does that build his or her confidence and character?

It doesn't. Athletes perform best when they feel they can be themselves, express themselves fully to their teammates and coaches, and focus on the task at hand: making tackles, blocking shots, and hitting home runs.

Many people in sports get that. Miami Dolphins owner Stephen Ross, whose team was at the epicenter of the Incognito-Martin controversy, told me there is a lot of history behind the locker room culture, and that history has to change.

"Everybody knows this wasn't unique to the Miami Dol-phins," Ross said. "If you played ball in school you know what it's like in the locker room. And a lot of it isn't paved with bad intentions, but it's something we have to learn from, how to treat people with respect and what it leads to, some of the social prob-lems in our country. And I think this will open people's eyes and I think we will do something very positive."

Successful college coaches get it too. When Gordon came out to UMass head basketball coach Derek Kellogg, the coach made it clear to his player: if anyone had a problem with Gordon, they could transfer to another school. Gordon wasn't going anywhere.

To show his support publicly for his newly out player, Kellogg explained at that time, "As a coaching staff, a team, and a family, we stressed to him that we support him in every way possible. Derrick is a first-class representative of this university and this program since he joined us and we are all very proud of him." (Gordon transferred to Seton Hall University a year later, but that had nothing to do with the acceptance of his sexual orientation by his coach.)

There's still a long way to go. Major pro sports leagues in Amer-ica count about five thousand athletes among their ranks. The coaches of these teams are among the most professional, most scrutinized people in their sports. At the high school level, where young men and women learn their behaviors, there are about 7.5 million athletes and hundreds of thousands of coaches, many of whom are unprofessional and poorly trained.

While so much of the public's attention is focused on those Sunday afternoons in autumn, it's the Friday-night lights that de-serve the scrutiny. More athletes will play high school football in Texas *this year* than will play in the entire NFL *over the next decade*. Hell, there are almost as many high school football *teams* in Texas as there are *players* in the National Football League.

Gordon wasn't pushed deep into the closet of isolation and depression by the atmosphere in pro sports. It was the casual homophobia of his teammates in his high school locker room, amplified by their college experience with coaches who turned a blind eye. It's the lower levels of sports that need our attention most, despite the glitz and glamor of pro sports and their resident celebrities.

This makes the visibility of athletes and the perpetual sharing of their stories in the mainstream media far more important. The more out athletes there are, the more coaches—particularly in high school and college—will realize they too may have a gay athlete on their team.

In 2011, University of Southern Maine baseball pitcher James Nutter stood in his bathroom with a bottle of pills in his hand, staring into the mirror. He had downed a dozen shots of whiskey to drown out the emotional pain of his predicament: he was gay in a sports world of straight people. Nutter's friends were his extended family. He judged his own self-worth by how those friends viewed him.

From the way they tossed around homophobia—"fucking faggots"—Nutter knew they wouldn't take kindly to him being something other than straight. He'd been naked with them. He'd showered with them. How would they react if it came out that he wanted to have sex with men, even if he never thought of his friends in that way? After years of inadvertent torment, he thought—he knew—he would lose all of his friends and would be suddenly, inextricably alone.

"It just got to the point where the paranoia of getting outed, and the culmination of all the stress of everything, clouded my judgment big time," James said. "My thought process snowballed. I developed this intense anxiety from trying to hide my sexuality from a lot of people. It got out of control, and I felt I couldn't handle it."

Nutter stood in his childhood home, his parents watching TV downstairs, crying into the mirror, ready to end his life. Better to be dead than shunned and alone.

Nutter didn't kill himself that day. He found the courage to set down the bottle of pills, head downstairs, and come out to his parents instead. In the following months, he would come out to his friends and, yes, even his teammates. Like so many before him, the guys who had said the worst things about gay people were the first ones to embrace him and convey their love.

When Nutter's former head coach at the University of Southern Maine, Ed Flaherty, heard that James was gay, he remembered a time when he defended a kid for saying "faggot" on the baseball diamond—it was, after all, just boys being boys. Flaherty could only imagine what had gone through Nutter's head as his coach essentially defended the use of a gay slur.

"Goddarnit," Flaherty said in his patented Maine accent after a long pause. "No matter what you win, you want those kids to be okay. Every once in a while there's a kid where you say, goddarn, could you have done more? Could you have helped? I'm fifty-nine years old. You start to think about these things a lot more than you did when you were twenty-nine. You don't realize what these kids are going through."

After learning his former player was gay, Flaherty stopped allowing homophobic slurs on the University of Southern Maine baseball team.

## Straight Guys Look Too

*I had sex with a straight man once.* He dated women, had a girlfriend. We met through work when I was a development executive at Disney just a year or so after starting *Outsports*. We bonded over our love of college basketball and one afternoon were sitting around my apartment in Los Angeles watching an NBA game. I don't know how it started or who started it, but somehow the conversation turned to sex. I won't dive too far into the details, but one thing led to another. Like it does.

When we finished, he cried. He said he had wondered about sex with another guy, but he always told himself he couldn't explore it. Jesus, the Bible, masculinity, the whole "gay guys don't do sports" thing—he offered up insightful yet all-too-familiar thoughts on his own internal homophobia with which I had once struggled. He left my apartment shortly after a quick handshake, quite shaken. As he walked out the door I knew I'd lost a friend to the secret truth so many straight men carry to their graves.

He called two weeks later, looking to hang out again. It was then I realized a powerful distinction: he hadn't cried in my apartment that day because he hated his sexual experience with me; he cried because he didn't.

It's that same mindset that drives most of the homophobia in locker rooms—particularly men's locker rooms. It's homophobia in the truest sense, an actual fear of homosexuality. Most everything else is rationalization.

Sure, some people have moral objections to gay sex, usually based on the Bible. But even devout Christians like Kurt Warner, Landry Jones, and Michael Irvin, who say they live their lives first and foremost for God, find ways to open their hearts to gay people and gay teammates. While some of these men may continue to oppose the idea of same-sex marriage or believe homosexuality is a sin, they understand that a locker room is made up of divergent beliefs, of which theirs is just one. Morality and the Bible are the rationalizations, not the reasons, for so many people saying they don't want gays in the locker room.

You can't welcome dog killers, child beaters, and rapists while claiming some moral objection to a teammate loving another man.

"Simple things, as far as showers and things like that, you know, of course, anyone would be uncomfortable," Adrian Peterson said in 2013. Why would someone like Peterson, who says he'd welcome a gay teammate, assume discomfort because there's an out gay man in the shower?

The fear we hear about most behind locker room attitudes is a disgust of being "looked at naked" by a teammate who happens to be gay. We hear this mostly from the men. They don't carry a fear of being raped or touched; no rational person thinks that's going to happen in a locker room surrounded by an entire team. Instead, these men are worried that their naked bodies will be simply seen by the eyes of a gay man. There's an odd subconscious feeling by some straight men that if they're "looked at" or "hit on" by gay men, being on the receiving end of that simple act somehow undermines their own heterosexuality and masculinity—that the innocent gaze of a gay man, gone unrejected, subjects the straight athlete to questions about himself. Some of those questions may even come loudest from his own mind.

I've talked to a lot of straight professional athletes about the idea of having a gay teammate. Almost universally these athletes say they would be fine with having someone gay on the team. Yet many of them couch it with a "as long as he knows how to behave" or "as long as he doesn't hit on me" disclaimer. Straight athletes feel the need to stereotype and reject gay teammates even in the same breath they use to accept them.

"I know I wouldn't be able to control myself if I were in a women's locker room," goes the drumbeat from many straight male athletes. Yes, you would. If you were changing with a bunch of women you would not launch into some uncontrolled sexual frenzy. You might make catcalls, whip their butts with wet towels, and joke about their junk out of discomfort—exactly what you do with the naked men with whom you shower.

Shortly after I came out to my close friends in Los Angeles, I was on the phone with my father. He was a state high school champion in the high jump when he was a teenager—he could hit his elbow on the basketball rim (at a time when dunking was illegal). I hadn't yet told him I was gay—in fact, I had just gotten out of a yearlong relationship with my girlfriend from college. For some reason on that call he launched into a series of jokes about gay men.

"What do you call a gay dentist?" he asked. I was stunned and couldn't fathom a guess. "A tooth fairy."

I dipped my toe in the topic on that phone call, and my dad told me what he had said several times before: "If a gay guy ever hit on me, I'd punch him in the face."

What's the big fear of being looked at by a gay person? Why do some straight men feel their masculinity—their very heterosexuality—will be questioned if a gay teammate sees his penis in the shower, or if a gay man at a club tells him he looks handsome that night? Are these men afraid of a pack of gay wolves lurking in corners of locker rooms, ready to pounce on unsuspecting straight athletes if they allow a gay man to look at them? Are they afraid a casual glance will somehow turn into more? Hardly.

Like my straight friend that day in my apartment, they're afraid of what it means if they don't mind it.

So many men who are seen naked by gay men, or who are hit on by other men, don't react because they're sickened by the thought, they react because they're afraid of what it means if they *aren't* sickened. These are men who want to be adored for their body—how it looks and what it can do in competition. They crave the attention, yet they need to put up a front of masculinity, couching their acceptance of nudity around a gay teammate with disclaimers. *#NoHomo.*

For a man confident in his sexuality, there's no issue. He knows he's straight. His teammates know he's straight. And if someone doesn't know he's straight or thinks he's not, he doesn't much care.

The rejection of gay men in the locker room isn't primarily about the Bible or even the gay man himself, it's about the lenses through which they are viewed and how people truly feel about themselves in the recesses of their subconscious.

Incidentally, my dad is now a vocal champion for gay rights. Like so many current and former athletes, he's come to a common conclusion: "What the hell was I so worried about?"

To be sure, gay guys look. Wade Davis, the openly gay man who attended training camps with three NFL teams, remembers one particular teammate who would put Dirk Diggler to shame. When I've been in locker rooms as a reporter, I've certainly noticed the naked bodies of athletes. I haven't looked per se, but I've noticed. You can't help it. With someone standing in front of you naked, it's hard not to notice their naked body, particularly given how much energy society expends covering it up.

*See! That Davis guy is gay and he was looking at other guys' cocks! And that reporter Zeigler should be banned from locker rooms! This proves you can't trust gay guys in the showers!*

Except . . . straight guys look too.

Jason Whitlock—the feisty on-and-off ESPN and Fox sports personality once known as "The Big Sexy"—remembers a player on his Ball State football team whom all the guys called "Kick Stand." And it wasn't because he rode his bicycle to practice.

This isn't just anecdotal. In 2014 two academics—Dr. Christopher Morriss-Roberts and Dr. Keith Gilbert—set out to explore the inner workings of sports locker rooms. They found that—shocker—all of the male athletes they spoke to, gay and straight, looked at other men's penises in the locker room. They didn't just look, they sized up the other men—they observed them, they watched them. And get this: the study found that men with larger penises became more popular in the locker room—straight athletes gravitated more toward them. The large penises were sources of social engagement as athletes would, like the Ball State football team, create nicknames for their well-hung teammates.

They didn't just look, they didn't just observe, they engaged! They wanted to be around the men with bigger dicks. They revered them.

Locker rooms are not sexual environments despite the fascination of the milieu in gay porn. They often stink, there's work to be done, everyone is there to do his job. Yet that atmosphere in locker rooms is often homoerotic. Men look at the bodies of other men to measure themselves against their peers. They do it to puff out their chests, like a peacock showing off his brilliant tail feathers. Men with big penises get a kick out of strutting around the locker room showing off their dominance over the other guys. It's less about sex than it is about competition and vulnerability.

It's entirely likely that gay men actually study their teammates' naked bodies less than their straight counterparts do. Openly gay former NFL defensive tackle Esera Tuaolo remembers consciously looking away from naked teammates so his true identity wouldn't be discovered—if he just didn't look at the other guys around him, there was less chance they would realize he was gay. Openly gay athletes often look away from their teammates lest they make them feel uncomfortable. Gay athletes in the study by Morriss-Roberts and Gilbert reported being more shy in the locker room than straight athletes.

Yes, gay athletes act less "gay" in the showers than do their straight counterparts.

Google *Anthony Davis spanking*. You'll find a twenty-second video of NBA star Anthony Davis while he was with the Kentucky Wildcats. The video features a naked Davis with only a towel around his waist. He's rolling on the ground laughing as a teammate tries to take the towel off him. When the teammate gets Davis's bare butt, he spanks it. Davis laughs throughout the video, even saying, "I love it." The team gathers around, laughing and celebrating the naked horseplay.

Men want this kind of interaction with other men. Have you ever wondered why gang showers are so common in men's locker rooms? Why bathhouses—where men go to be naked with one another—have been popular since before the Roman Empire? Our modern-day American locker rooms have replaced those bathhouses. The male desire to be naked with other men has not changed. Sure, the puritanical laws of American culture have put a damper on nudity. While men in some cultures have embraced nude beaches and skimpy swimsuits, American culture has pushed to demasculinize the naked male body and driven us to hide any hint of our penises with baggy pants and shorts. As our culture becomes more aware of its sexuality, that is shifting.

Yet the desire to be naked with teammates and friends, to

horseplay, has not gone away. It has been buried beneath the sur-
face of our public conversations, forced into the dark corners of
our culture. It has been in those dark corners of fraternity houses, the
military, police departments, and locker rooms that it has reared
its ugly head in another far less healthy form.

The institution of hazing goes back decades, if not centuries. Hazing is, for all intents and purposes, the initiating of new members
into a group (or onto a team) by making them do crazy shit they
wouldn't otherwise ever choose to do without pressure.

The rationalization behind it is twofold. First, new initiates
into a group need to break through some kind of barrier—pass
a test—if they want to be part of a group. The recruits need to
understand there's a pecking order and they're at the bottom of
it. On a sports team, the veterans had to go through these hoops
when they were rookies, so now they're going to do it to the next
batch of rookies who need to learn "their place." They need to
fight for a spot in the brotherhood . . . by getting naked, drinking
alcohol, being spanked, and allowing themselves to be dunked in
ice water.

The other rationalization for hazing claims there are certain
situations that are such pressure-cookers that some kind of "bonding" is mandated. The military, college fraternities, and sports
teams all utilize this need for bonding to defend their behaviors,
as though forcing new recruits to get naked and jerk off onto a
cracker will somehow help them compete together.

Makes perfect sense, right?

Yet what sports team has ever performed better because the
veterans hazed the rookies? When the New Orleans Saints hazed
their rookies in 1998 and nearly cost tight end Cam Cleeland his
vision, the team finished 6–10. The 2012–13 Sacramento Kings
finished with an abysmal .341 winning percentage, yet had pub-

licly hazed rookie Thomas Robinson (among others, I'm sure). Would people really argue that the prolonged success of the New England Patriots and San Antonio Spurs is because the captains of those teams simply know how to haze better than the Jacksonville Jaguars and Washington Wizards?

Every reason offered up to defend the ritual of hazing— bonding, the need to win, initiation—is undermined when real facts and results come to light. A professional sports team's goal is to win games, yet hazing has absolutely no measurable effect on a team's ability to do so. The same holds for college and high school teams. If team leadership—from the coaches to the captains— needs to employ a practice of dunking players in vats of ice or stripping them nude and forcing them to sing a song in front of the team, then that leadership cannot claim to be effective. Embarrassing rookies and freshmen is no replacement for leadership. Hazing has never led to a single tackle, a single basket, or a single win in the history of sports. Yet our culture celebrates the concept of hazing despite its sometimes dire consequences.

"And hazing, you gotta love it." Those were the words of ESPN host Trey Wingo in August 2005 when *NFL Live* aired a video of Carolina Panthers veterans hazing a rookie at training camp by taping him to a goal post. Wingo and the other commentators laughed and joked about the practice. Nowhere in the conversation was there any talk of the dangers of what we were seeing on the TV screen. When I chastised the men for celebrating hazing, I received a stern phone call from Wingo, who was apoplectic that I would infer he supported the practice of hazing that could potentially lead to someone sodomizing teenagers.

In fairness, I don't think Wingo or anyone else at ESPN would in any way consciously endorse the darker sides of hazing. (In fact, Wingo has become a powerful voice at ESPN on behalf of LGBT people.) Yet they enthusiastically and very publicly support these "innocuous" actions that lead down a more destructive path, particularly for youth. If hazing was truly innocuous, no one would engage in it.

What hazing does is harm the new initiates. Soon after the Dallas Cowboys drafted wide receiver Dez Bryant, the team went out to dinner. They ran up a $55,000 tab, all charged to the rookie. Harmless, right? No one got hurt? Except Bryant was out enough cash for a potential down payment on his mother's new home. He resented his teammates for it. It drove a wedge between them, with Bryant publicly declaring he would not be hazed anymore. Veterans fired back publicly that, oh yes, he would be. ESPN's Matt Mosley referred to a previous incident in which Bryant had refused to carry a veteran teammate's shoulder pads as "innocent" hazing. The Cowboys ended that season with a 6–10 record.

More often than you could possibly believe, hazing leads to forced nudity and sexual acts including sodomy, particularly in high school and college. Three players on the basketball team at Ooltewah High School in Tennessee decided to end 2015 by sodomizing one of their teammates in the name of hazing. Allegedly. Three high school football players in Missouri were arrested in early 2015 for sodomizing four younger players. Six members of New York State's Sayreville High School football team were arrested in 2014 for allegedly sexually assaulting teammates. In 2012, two Iowa high school wrestlers were charged with sodomizing young athletes with a jump rope handle. That's just a quick overview of examples in recent years plucked from big headlines. For every incident of hazing rape that gets reported, there are many more with victims who don't want to be branded with the stigma of sodomy.

A well-publicized episode involving Mepham High School in Bellmore, New York was particularly telling. At a summer football camp in August 2003, team veterans sodomized younger players with broomsticks, golf balls, and pinecones. Pinecones! It came almost ten years after a player accused the coaching staff and several members of the same football program of a hazing attack that gave him a concussion—that case was settled out of court. After the 2003 incident, former players talked about the culture of Mepham coach Kevin McElroy's football team, and how hazing had been a part of it for many years. It had likely started out "harmless" before involving physical attacks. Incoming freshmen learned from the veterans that these things were part of being on the team; and when they became the veterans, the cycle continued down the slippery slope.

People who start out with good intentions can very quickly become wrapped up in sinister deeds. The Stanford Prison Experiment demonstrated that, with seemingly well-meaning young men turning into the pigs of *Animal Farm* within hours. The mentality that drives boys to sodomize freshmen is the same one that drives grown men to duct-tape other grown men to a chair on a field or force them to pay for a $55,000 dinner.

So why do we put up with hazing? Why do commentators on ESPN chuckle about it? Why are so many athletes caught up in the practice of forcing younger athletes into subservient roles involving nudity and sexual assault?

Because homophobia runs so deep in the subconscious of men in American culture that this is the only way many straight men can feel comfortable bonding at a literally naked level with other men: in the dark.

The arguments against gay men in the locker room revolve around gay men looking at their naked teammates, touching their teammates' butts or penises—doing things that, well, straight guys do with each other.

Yes, this stuff is already going on without openly gay athletes

in the room. Straight, bisexual, and closeted men are already doing everything anyone could possibly fear from gay teammates—
there is nothing a gay athlete could possibly do that isn't already
being exercised in the locker rooms of high school, college, and
professional sports teams from Mepham High School to the Miami Dolphins. Until it crosses a line, everybody's cool with it. It
can even cross the line and some men will still find the practice
perfectly acceptable. It's all okay because the men in the room
are all assumed to be straight; it's only horseplay. It's "boys being
boys."

Throw a gay man into that mix, and in the minds of many
straight athletes it becomes "boys being gay."

Adding an out gay man into a locker room changes the meaning of these "team bonding" exercises in the minds of men. Of
course, it doesn't change the actual meaning of anything. The desire for men to be naked with one another, to subject rookies
to embarrassing hazing incidents or smack each other with their
cocks in the shower (yes, straight guys actually do this), hasn't
changed. The only dynamic that shifts when a gay man is thrown
into the middle of that world is the meaning of those actions in
the minds of the people engaged in it.

Would the Kentucky Wildcats gather around and laugh as
a gay Anthony Davis rolled around the floor half-naked? Would
they touch his bare butt as he hollered, "I love it"? It's doubtful—
not necessarily because twenty-year-olds today have an issue with
gay people, but because of concerns over how their interaction
would be perceived by others. And even if they were spanking
an openly gay naked teammate, the evidence sure wouldn't have
ended up on YouTube. "Guilt by association" is a real fear for a
lot of athletes. If one person on a sports team is gay, the thinking
goes, then everyone on the team is gay. If you're friends with a gay
person, then your sexuality is in question—why, after all, would

you be friends with a gay person if you didn't want to have sex with them? "Gay by association."

This isn't a dynamic owned by the men. In fact, it can be even more complicated and powerful in women's sports. Because female athletes are sometimes assumed to be lesbians, many lesbian athletes feel pressure to stay in the closet lest they "indict" the entire team. There are powerful closeted lesbian coaches who encourage their players to stay in the closet so their entire program isn't dubbed a "lesbian" team.

Rival coaches use that information and that fear in a practice called "negative recruiting." College coaches will pray on the fear of lesbian athletes when visiting potential recruits and their families. "You don't want to go Stanford," the not-so-subtle conversation will go. "They don't have a traditional family environment." A lesbian might see you in the shower. Gasp!

Various players on the Stanford University women's basketball team have come out of the closet publicly, making the school a prime target of negative recruiting. Because of Stanford's strong academic reputation and the impressive track record of head coach Tara VanDerveer, the program is able to thrive and compete annually for a national title. No matter who comes out publicly in the Stanford women's basketball program, the team will continue to thrive. Yet the coaches and players of lower-profile teams struggle to fight against the "lesbian program" label that negative recruiting can dramatically generate.

This whole dynamic gets to the core of the issue for a lot of people, athletes or otherwise: What is it to be gay? How do you define a gay person? And how do elements in our society affect that oh-so-scary label?

For some, the scary part comes from the low threshold of defining someone as "gay." If you look at another dude's junk and don't immediately look away, you're gay. If you're not totally grossed out by the site of another guy's penis, you're gay. If kissing another guy or sucking somebody's dick has entered into the recesses of a dream as you were sleeping, you're gay. It's amazing how many men deny that last piece has happened to them, even though experts say it is not uncommon.

For others, the danger lies in simply being perceived as gay by friends and teammates. Again, gay is weak. If you're Kobe Bryant, you call someone "gay" to signify that they are wrong or stupid or weak. Deep in the subconscious, gay is bad. The last thing you want as a professional athlete is for your competitors or your teammates to view you as weak. Despite the growing list of strong, successful gay athletes—Esera Tuaolo, Jason Collins, Michael Sam—this perception persists.

Frankly, even the gay community isn't immune to it. Gay men use something called "bottom shaming" to marginalize other people as somehow more "gay" or more feminine than the more "masc" gay men. Bottoms are the, well, bottom of a sexual position— the guy being penetrated by the other. I've been asked a bunch of times if I was the "woman" in the relationship, meaning am I the "bottom." Fathers fear the idea of their son being the "bottom." Gay men use those sexist and homophobic stereotypes and labels to embarrass and marginalize one another. It's the same thing straight men do to each other.

The fear of being caught "looking" in the shower is closely related to all of this. Fears of perception, fears of labels, fears of femininity and weakness. It all lingers because straight men won't talk honestly about their lives and how they relate to homosexuality and homoeroticism. They hide their glances in the shower and turn inquisitive stares into "horseplay."

# Yes, Lots of Lesbians Play Elite Sports

**Advocates who decry the discrepancy** in media coverage for male athletes versus female athletes had a field day with the coming-out of WNBA star Brittney Griner and Jason Collins. Griner, who came out publicly less than two weeks before Collins in April 2013, got a small fraction of the attention her NBA counterpart received for his historic announcement.

To be sure, sexism in sports was a major part of it. The NBA's TV revenue is $2.67 billion per year, which is $2.66 billion more than the WNBA's annual TV revenue. In America, men's pro sports are king and the women suffer from inequality. Fewer opportunities exist for women as players, coaches, front-office executives, and sports journalists. Female athletes have had to fight hard for equal prize money in sports like tennis where the interest they draw from fans is equal or near equal to that of men. Sports—and in particular professional sports—exhibit a microcosm of sexism in this country at its most destructive, no doubt.

Yet there are other forces at play that drive more coverage for Collins's announcement than Griner's, that create more buzz for men coming out in sports than women. Most importantly, the idea of lesbians in sports simply isn't big news in 2015 and hasn't been for years; many more female athletes have already come out publicly.

To best understand the shrinking media coverage for the

coming-out of lesbian athletes, it's more informative to compare Griner to the public coming-out of Sheryl Swoopes.

Griner's news was the result of what she says was a surprise question in a post–WNBA draft *Sports Illustrated* video. The *SI* interviewer asked Griner about gay athletes, leaving the WNBA's No. 1 draft pick with nowhere to go but to share her sexual orientation right then and there. The news of Griner's revelation trickled out over the next few days. There was no *Sports Illustrated* cover, no publicist, no media strategy, no "big bang" designed to grab the public's attention.

When Swoopes came out publicly in 2005—eight years before Griner—she received an avalanche of media coverage. Like Griner, Swoopes was one of the big names in the WNBA at the time. Unlike Griner, Swoopes had a carefully orchestrated coming-out, complete with publicist Howard Bragman pulling the strings and media lined up to give the story a big push.

Yet even in 2005, when same-sex marriage was legal in exactly one state, even with Swoopes's big splash, few expressed surprise that there was a lesbian in women's professional basketball. Beyond the traditional stereotypes of female athletes, several WNBA players had already come out publicly, including Michele Van Gorp and Sue Wicks. "I can't say how many [WNBA] players are gay," Wicks told the *Village Voice* in 2000, "but it would be easier to count the straight ones."

While women weren't coming out publicly in droves, many people in the WNBA knew who was gay and who wasn't. Like Wicks said, lesbian basketball players were not a rarity in perception or reality, and fans and members of the media either knew it or suspected it. An NBA executive once admitted to me that there were serious conversations in the WNBA about how to handle the league's image as being full of lesbians in the 1990s.

"Is anyone really surprised that there's a lesbian in the

WNBA?" I was asked on multiple occasions in the days following Swoopes's announcement. *Ho hum.*

"It's never a surprise that there might be a gay person in sports," I responded in 2005. "But what is powerful about this is that one of the sport's biggest stars has found the courage to come out."

Swoopes was not only one of the league's best players, she was one of the greatest basketball players of all time. Not one of the best female players, but one of the best players. You can stack up her accolades—three MVPs, four WNBA rings, three Olympic golds—against almost any professional basketball player, man or woman. She had won the league's scoring title just before coming out in October 2005. Because of preconceived notions that "all female athletes are lesbians," we saw and heard various fans and experts dismissing Swoopes's revelation as mundane news despite few athletes with her pedigree ever coming out.

Yet the explosion of attention Swoopes's story received was more like that shown Collins than like the attention Griner received because 1) the announcement was orchestrated, and 2) a superstar actually coming out in women's basketball was still somewhat rare in 2005.

While Major League Soccer has only one out player—Robbie Rogers—and the 2014 Men's World Cup had zero publicly out participants, the 2015 Women's World Cup featured at least seventeen players and coaches who were publicly out. One anonymous source I spoke to before the Women's World Cup said she was personally aware of eighty women in the World Cup who were LGBT. The head coaches of the United States and Sweden— both top-five teams worldwide—were out lesbians, and both of the teams had at least three players who were out.

The NBA has had only two current or former players come out publicly—John Amaechi and Jason Collins. Yet it's nearly impossible to track all the out current and former women in the WNBA. Brittney Griner, Glory Johnson, Seimone Augustus, Janel McCarville, Cappie Pondexter, Sharnee Zoll-Norman, Angel McCoughtry, Layshia Clarendon, along with coaches like Pokey Chatman and Lin Dunn, have all come out publicly in the media or social media. And that's just a sampling.

At the 2012 Summer Olympic Games there were twenty-three publicly out LGBT athletes, twenty of whom were women. Only three men—Carl Hester and Edward Gal in equestrian and Matthew Mitcham in diving—had found their way publicly out of the closet.

With so few out athletes and coaches in men's professional sports, it's easy to understand why people believe that homophobia is still a powerful force in the NBA, MLB, NFL, and the like. Michael Sam is the consummate example of that, dropping down in the NFL draft and then struggling to find a team in part because he was publicly out. While the vast majority of fans and players have moved on, there is certainly an argument to be made that the older guys in suits who make the big decisions in the leagues are still stuck in the eighties.

Yet that question has been to some extent put to rest in the WNBA and women's professional soccer. There are numerous out lesbians across both sports, being drafted, traded, and acquired by teams with the knowledge that the athlete they are bringing onto the team is LGBT. When Griner—the league's most visible out lesbian—was awarded the WNBA's Defensive Player of the Year Award in 2014 and went on to win the league title with the Phoenix Mercury that same season, she demonstrated that out lesbians aren't just playing in the league, they are succeeding and winning awards by popular vote. Seimone Augustus proved the same point after coming out, then being named all-WNBA first team in 2012 and an All-Star Game starter in 2013. Abby Wambach and Megan Rapinoe—both out lesbians in professional soccer—are two of the biggest American names in their sport and were darlings of the media and fans after their 2015 World Cup title.

The situation in many individual sports isn't much different. No major male professional tennis player has ever come out publicly in the modern era, yet some of the greatest female players of all time have done so: Billie Jean King, Martina Navratilova, Amelie Mauresmo, Gigi Fernandez, Lisa Raymond, and Rennae Stubbs, to name just a few.

Men's pro sports are stuck where women's pro sports were in the early eighties, with athletes still afraid of losing endorsement deals and being cut from their teams. Meanwhile, women's pro sports are more firmly entrenched in the modern era, with a large swath of out lesbians sporting endorsement deals and winning big-time awards.

With all of that said, there is still fear. The vast majority of lesbian pro athletes and coaches choose to stay silent.

I mentioned earlier the dismissive "why is a lesbian in sports a story" question I got a lot when Swoopes came out. Over the years that's been slowly replaced by another question that helps reveal why the vast majority of lesbian professional athletes don't come out publicly.

"Isn't it easy for women to come out in sports?"

On the one hand the question is faulty. What it's really getting at is whether it's easy to BE a lesbian in sports, not whether it's easy to come out. It's hard to say almost any woman has it "easy" in sports. To get equal airtime a female athlete has to be Serena Williams, one of the greatest athletes of all time. If she's "just" WNBA player Candace Parker, she gets virtually ignored by the media and public at large. Parker's base salary as the WNBA's No. 1 draft pick in 2008 was about $44,000; the salary of Derrick

Rose, the NBA's top pick that year, was $4.8 million—about 110 times that of Parker.

Female athletes don't have it "easy" in pro sports. Period.

"That's the danger in women's sports," Indiana Fever guard Layshia Clarendon told me. "The 'everyone's a lesbian' idea makes you think it's totally free of homophobia. But it's not."

It's hard to say that *any* LGBT people have it "easy" in America, even in 2016. We still live in a culture where children are raised to be straight, expected to be straight, the overwhelming majority of messages from the media point to a straight culture (while gay people cling to the few positive messages we see on TV), churches and the Republican Party routinely target LGBT people and their rights in dehumanizing ways, and while the sports media has shifted its tone toward positive portrayals of LGBT athletes, there is still a sense of "other" to it.

No, it isn't easy to be a lesbian in sports.

Yet it's also illuminating to acknowledge a difference in sports—and in our broader culture—between the experiences of lesbians and gay men. There are factors that mitigate some of the barriers for lesbians in professional sports that are still paramount for gay athletes in elite men's sports.

The support structures are incomparable. As soon as a lesbian comes out in professional sports—and many college sports teams—she often has other lesbian players or coaches on her team or within shouting distance who are out or at least willing to be part of her circle of confidantes. The statistics don't lie: lesbians are represented throughout college and professional sports. When the Board of Trustees at Erskine College attempted to adopt an anti-gay policy at the school, one athlete told me, "There goes the entire women's sports program." And that's at a small religious school in South Carolina.

Gay men in sports simply don't have that immediate access

to other athletes like them. Statistics certainly would claim that any Division I college football team has at least one gay player. Other sports may be more likely to attract gay men—more gay male college swimmers have come out publicly than in any other sport. Yet by all accounts, the number of gay men out or prepared to come out in college and professional sports is dwarfed by the number of lesbians. Twenty years from now that dynamic will be drastically different as a steady stream of athletes keep coming out, but today there's a huge discrepancy between the genders.

But the question that keeps getting asked is about coming out. Is it easier to come out in women's sports than in men's sports?

The ease of coming out has nothing to do with someone's gender because the fear of coming out is generally irrational. Emotion is irrational. Fear is irrational. And the biggest hurdle anyone thinking about coming out has to clear is fear—specifically, fear of the unknown. How will my parents react? What will my coach say? Will my endorsement deal with Adidas get renewed? So many of these questions have been answered over and over again in the last decade by Swoopes and Griner and Augustus and Rapinoe and so many others coming out publicly and being embraced.

While these facts are rational, fear is not.

By every account I have tried to measure, there is a preponderance of lesbians in elite-level team sports. The old stereotype that every female athlete is a lesbian certainly isn't accurate—but within some stereotypes there is an ounce of truth.

When I interviewed Portland Thorns player Meleana Shim in 2013, she was very casual about the number of lesbians in her sport. Only a small handful of female professional soccer players had come out publicly before her, and Shim wanted to change that by setting an example for them.

"I feel like there are a lot of gay women in soccer," she told me. "But not very many of us openly talk about it. I think now more of us are starting to take a stand, but I still don't think it's very representative of just how many of us there are. I think the silence sends a message that it's not okay to be a lesbian in sports."

While I didn't print her best guess at the time, Shim estimated that about half of the women she knew in American professional soccer were gay or bisexual.

Months later I was the guest of a class about sports journalism at USC with then–*Yahoo! Sports* producer and content editor Kari Van Horn. Having been in and around the Los Angeles sports scene for years as a USC grad herself, Van Horn had spent time with the Los Angeles Sparks and covering the WNBA in general. She told me something that night that changed my world: "Over a third of the WNBA is gay," she said. "I know these women. There are a lot of them."

I didn't know. I think part of me wanted to remain blind to it. Stereotypes had held a lot of power over me as a gay man, particularly when I was a kid. A third of the WNBA being gay meant that a majority were still not LGBT, so it's not like the number brought great validation to the stereotype. Still, when about 4 percent of the population identifies in a census as gay and possibly as many as 33 percent of the athletes in a particular sport are lesbians, that says a lot about who is attracted to the sport at the most elite level.

Then Van Horn hit me with another stat: "And I know for a fact that some teams are more than half lesbian."

When I talked with a closeted women's college basketball coach shortly after the 2015 Final Four, she told me that 85 percent of the other female college basketball coaches she knew were lesbians. That's about seven out of eight. The number seemed exceptionally high, so I ran the thought by former Portland State University women's basketball head coach Sherri Murrell.

"I think that's a pretty accurate number, give or take a few," Murrell said.

Layshia Clarendon said that on every team she's been a part of, they count the number of lesbians. "Okay, seven of us are gay and one of us is bi. And one has slept with a woman, but she's straight. So we have 8.5. It's a thing to see where the balance is, to see if we're more of a gay thing or a straight thing."

In 2016, it's imposssible to imagine many men's sports teams going through the same exercise with similar ease and honesty.

While female athletes experience an environment more open to different sexual orientations, the same is not true for lesbian coaches.

In 1972, when Title IX was implemented to build equal access to sports for female college athletes, 90 percent of women's college teams had a woman as a head coach, according to a study by the University of Minnesota. Forty years later, only 40 percent of women's teams were being helmed by a woman—less than half. While opportunities have increased for female athletes, they have plunged for female coaches.

As women are being passed over for coaching positions in women's sports, they aren't even considered for coaching spots on men's teams. A 2012 study by Acosta and Carpenter from Brooklyn College found that between 2 and 3.5 percent of men's college teams had female head coaches.

Doubters can certainly point to exceptions. When the San Antonio Spurs hired Becky Hammon as an assistant coach in August 2014, the organization made a powerful statement about the future of female coaches in men's pro sports. The Arizona Cardinals brought in Jen Welter for a preseason coaching internship in July 2015. Tennis player Andy Murray famously hired out lesbian Amelie Mauresmo as his coach in 2014, resulting in his first-ever title on clay courts and his first victory on clay over the legendary Rafael

Nadal. Women certainly have opportunities to coach men's sports.

Yet these are exceptions, not the rule.

The barring of women from coaching men at the college or professional levels is rooted in deep-seated sexism. But it's hard to point exclusively to sexism when diving into the decline in opportunities for women coaching women. Sexism and homophobia educate one another, and in few cases is that more clear than the fear lesbian coaches face in landing their next job.

The old-boys club is hard at work promoting from within. While the discrepancy of male-to-female college coaches is a professional disgrace, it's easy to see how it develops. Sports institutions are too often given a pass on professionalism. The locker room is deemed a unique space where elements of homophobia, sexism, and poor decorum are allowed to run rampant. Often more fraternity house than boardroom, sports teams and athletic departments at various levels are given a pass—or at least the benefit of a blind eye—to avoid "distractions" that might make people uncomfortable. What does that look like? Too often those male athletic directors are made uncomfortable by powerful women in coaching or sports-administration positions.

"I watch our athletic director interact with men in our program," a closeted basketball coach said of her male athletic director in early 2015. "There's more eye contact [when he talks to the men] and more depth to the conversations. He spends more time with them."

With men occupying 80 percent of college athletic director positions and 74 percent of college president seats, it should be no surprise that women are being pushed out of the coaching ranks. With the rising tide against female coaches, it's also no wonder lesbians in the profession are so afraid to come out.

Recruiting can be half of the job description for college coaches. When a coach enters a recruit's home and sits down with her parents to discuss her future, the entire program is on display: facilities, scholarships, location, and yes, the personal lives of the coaches and players. For many recruits, the sexual orientation of players and coaches isn't a concern. Yet it's not the recruits who often have the most problematic questions—it's the parents. The persistent stereotype that lesbians are "recruiting" young women to become gay is a powerful distortion that preys on the fears many parents have for their children.

"If I have to go up against a straight male it's a concern, particularly if it's brought up as a concern by the parents," a Division I women's basketball assistant coach told me. Sherri Murrell, the former head coach of the Portland State women's basketball team, said very clearly that she believes she lost recruits because she was an out lesbian. The issue is widespread and serious, and the NCAA has tried to tackle it with surface-level solutions like panel discussions and the development of resources to combat negative recruiting based on sexual orientation. Yet the problem hasn't gone away.

That fear of the public's reaction to female coaches took a toll on University of Minnesota–Duluth women's ice hockey coach Shannon Miller. Despite winning five national championships from 2001 to 2010, Miller claims she was routinely pushed out of public events like fundraisers and athletic-department functions. When the nameplate outside her office door was defaced with the slur *Dyke,* Miller says administrators repeatedly failed to replace the plaque; she ultimately replaced it herself. "There's no doubt in my mind that homophobia is one of the factors as to why I've been treated so poorly by some in the UMD athletic department," she said.

Miller was released from her job in 2015 when the team finished ninth nationally. (The school cited budget cuts, even though she earned a far lower salary than the way less successful men's ice hockey coach.) She was replaced by another female coach, but the school had little choice given Miller's impending federal lawsuit—claiming sexism and homophobia—and the very public outcry against the firing of female coaches that their move generated.

Miller has not been able to secure a coaching job since her firing, despite her track record. The same holds for other lesbian coaches like Lisa Howe, who was fired by Belmont University for telling her soccer team that she and her partner were expecting a child. She was let go despite a winning record of 52–48–16 and this exemplary statement by the university on her 2010 online bio: *The program has not only soared on the field but continues to excel in the classroom under Howe's leadership.*

While countless female athletes at the professional and collegiate level have been able to come out publicly with little backlash, coaches have not had that luxury. Largely gone are the days when Penn State's women's basketball coach Rene Portland was allowed to have a "no lesbians" policy (though two Pepperdine University basketball players are suing the school and women's basketball coach over an alleged "no lesbians" policy). Yet the impact of that type of unspoken bigotry is growing for lesbian coaches across college sports.

One powerful way to combat all of this would be for a large group of lesbian coaches to come out publicly together at the same time. Many gay people, including Howe, have expressed a desire to keep their private lives out of the media spotlight while at the same time inspiring other LGBT people to be true to themselves. A mass coming-out would diffuse the public attention and maximize the liberating impact on people in the closet. The media has about a forty-eight-hour attention span for these things; if a dozen women's coaches all came out at the same time on various media outlets, most likely none of them would get more than a sprinkle of individual focus.

It's an idea Murrell and I have explored in various conversations. The fear, sadly, runs too deep. Murrell can't get any traction for the idea despite knowing dozens of lesbian coaches, many of whom are out at least partially to their team or staff.

I have heard secondhand reports of one closeted Division I head coach, whose job and legacy are in no jeopardy, encouraging her lesbian players to stay in the closet because "sports are no place for one's personal life." It's the mantra of a bygone generation directly impacting the lives of young, impressionable lesbians.

So the cycle continues.

The decisions of (mostly male) athletic directors to diminish the number of opportunities for female coaches is deeply problematic. Yet there are female coaches—many of them lesbians, according to Murrell and others—being hired by schools. Unfortunately, however, the opportunity to change the dynamic in women's sports is blunted, in part because almost all of these coaches choose to keep that aspect of themselves hidden from the public.

Layshia Clarendon was well aware of all of this—the fears and the hurdles women and lesbians face in sports—when she approached her senior season with the Cal Bears in 2012. She had found a family on the team, straight women who embraced and respected her, along with lesbian teammates to bond with and learn from. The coaching staff and players welcomed her girlfriend to games. When she decided to sport a mohawk and dye it golden, it was a powerful statement of individuality that, Clarendon said, resonated with other lesbians in the sport. Cal was "such a safe space" for her.

Yet she wanted to do more. Visibility, she knew, was a key—lesbians were all over college basketball, and she didn't want any struggling teen to think otherwise. As Cal prepared for their run at a national championship, she and a teammate wanted to make

March "LGBT Awareness Month" for her team and her sport.
There was Breast Cancer Awareness Month, so why not this?

So, headed into the 2013 NCAA tournament, Clarendon and
her teammate painted rainbows on their basketball shoes as another symbol of inclusion. They had found a home at Cal and
wanted to make sure other women knew they could be their true
selves there. The Bears were a No. 2 seed with a high national
profile that year; Clarendon intended to use the opportunity of
higher visibility to make a statement.

From the same coaching staff and administration who had
shown so much support for their lesbian players, Clarendon suddenly felt concern. What would be the external repercussions of
their players being so publicly out about their sexual orientation?
Other schools had suffered from being labeled as having a "lesbian
program." Could that ultimately hurt Cal's rising status? Clarendon told me they also worried about whether their star guard was
ready for the possible implications of her multicolored sneakers.

Clarendon said a meeting was called to talk about the
repercussions of her choice of hairstyle.

"Hey, I have a mohawk," Clarendon told them. "I'm obviously
very prepared for what having a rainbow on my shoe means."

While her hair had been the talk of the media, the rainbow on
the shoes was largely ignored—the source of concern never mate-
rialized. Yet the episode was an important lesson for Clarendon.
Even within the family, with all of the support people had shown
her at Cal, there still seemed to be some institutional fear of
having a star player loudly and proudly literally wearing rainbows.

This has made visibility as an out LGBT athlete all the more
important for Clarendon.

# Tony Dungy and "Muscular Christians" Use the Bible to Commit Abominations

**Six weeks after Tony Dungy** led the Indianapolis Colts to their Super Bowl title in 2007, the coach stood before the Indiana Family Institute and delivered a speech of praise. The IFI is an organization created specifically to attack social-justice advances for LGBT people, wrapping everything they do around the Bible and placing their perceived Word of God ahead of the American values of liberty and freedom.

The Institute was honoring Dungy at its annual dinner for two main reasons. As a devout Christian, Dungy has put God front-and-center for much of his public life. After the Colts won the Super Bowl, Dungy said, "The Lord orchestrated this," as though God had deemed the Colts more worthy of that year's world title than the Chicago Bears and New England Patriots, their final two opponents. "My purpose in life is simply to glorify God," Dungy once said. "I coach football. But the good I can do to glorify God along the way is my real purpose."

The second and far more obvious reason the IFI chose Dungy as their keynote speaker for that dinner was to raise money. They didn't feature a small-town Sunday school teacher who had dedicated forty years of her life to educating children and feeding the poor, they picked the guy who was the toast of Indiana and who would help sell tickets. Dungy's purpose at that dinner was to raise money for the organization's efforts to fight against the rights of gay people. He did just that.

In the lead-up to the event a firestorm brewed. Was Dungy really going to headline an event designed to raise money to fight against equality for gay people? The IFI was using an image of Dungy in Colts regalia to promote his appearance—was the Colts organization endorsing the actions of this group? Dungy was publicly silent until his appearance at the fundraiser when he made it crystal clear that he supported the organization's work against same-sex marriage and other issues.

"I appreciate the stance they're taking," Dungy said in his remarks, "and I embrace that stance."

Dungy went on to explain that his perspective was shaped by the Word of God. "IFI is saying what the Lord says," Dungy told the audience. "You can take that and make your decision on which way you want to be. I'm on the Lord's side . . . We're trying to promote the family—family values the Lord's way."

Let's distill this into its key elements: 1) Tony Dungy, celebrated coach of the Colts, raised thousands of dollars for an anti-gay organization 2) whose policies he embraces because 3) it's the Word of God. It paints a pretty clear picture that's no different from the one athletes, coaches, and most people in America have come to expect from devout Christians.

*Do not lie with a man as with a woman; it is an abomination.*

That one line in the Holy Bible has caused more harm for gays and lesbians than a hundred thousand swords. The New International Version of the Holy Bible is a thousand pages, give or take, yet this one verse buried in a book called Leviticus, along with literally just a few more words, has given license to generations of people to shun, torment, and even kill gay people in the name of God.

The Bible, and in particular the Old Testament, lays out a lifestyle in which homosexuality is wrong, a sin, an "abomination." People can slice and dice the words, twisting them and interpreting them as they want. Various scholars have. At Stanford, one of my religious studies professors explained that that passage only pertained to straight people; somehow, there was an alternate set of rules for gay people, that this "sin" expressed explicitly in Leviticus didn't pertain to me because I don't lie with my partner the way I would a woman. Not even I buy that one.

We can spin these arguments around and around. The fact of the matter is, many in the church—like Dungy and the IFI—have made homosexuality a sin from which fornicators must be saved. That mantra has spilled into sports in a powerful way. Christianity has a death grip on so many athletes and coaches from high school to the pros. NFL teams have chaplains to bless them and lead Bible study. High school basketball teams pray together before their games. Baseball players signal the Hail Mary before they step up to bat.

Outside of the military, the two most traditionally homophobic corners of American culture are commonly thought to be sports and religion. When the two collide—when the clergy meet the coach—the subtle message to gay athletes isn't generally one of inclusion. While both institutions are changing—in some corners faster than others—because of the decades-long anti-gay mantras of these two worlds, it takes proactive leaders to change both the perception and the reality.

I know a gay NFL player who was on the Colts. It was after Dungy had left the team, but it helps to elucidate the point: in all likelihood there was a gay player on the Colts under Dungy, whether it was this particular player or not. Put yourself in his cleats. Imagine watching your head coach raise money for an anti-gay organization and hearing him embrace the group's positions, all in the name of God. You've heard for the better part of two decades that the sports world and the church reject you, that you don't belong. And now your head coach raises money to fight against your equality since you are an abomination. After all, that is the Bible's version of the Word of God.

How could a gay athlete or coach possibly find fulfillment in that environment? Despite inclusion policies touted by the NFL and NFLPA, how could a gay person possibly feel—in Dungy's locker room and coaches' offices—that he could ever express fully who he is?

Dungy is one of the most extreme publicly anti-gay examples of religion in athletics, but make no mistake: Religion. Is. Everywhere. In. Sports.

It's plastered across the Twitter feed of Seattle Seahawks quarterback Russell Wilson. *Jesus follower* are the first two words on his permanent profile. He often quotes Bible verses. When he wins a big football game, he thanks God on television.

Tim Tebow, winner of the Heisman Trophy and two national college football championships, painted a Bible verse on his eye black before every game. It got so bad that the NCAA adopted rule 1.4.6e: "Any shading under a player's eyes must be solid black with no words, numbers, logos, or other symbols." Tebow famously prayed after every touchdown and held a prayer on the field with players from both teams after every game in college and the NFL.

Ron Brown, assistant football coach at Nebraska, preached the Bible to players, held Bible studies and prayer sessions, and spoke publicly against any protection for gay people because, like Dungy, God told him to.

The marriage between sports and Christianity is nothing new. Since the 1800s there's been a push by religious leaders in America to use sports as a tool for recruiting and empowering young men into the Christian church. "Muscular Christianity" became an entire movement in the late nineteenth century to build an army of strong, athletic men indoctrinated in Christian culture to take leadership roles in the church and society at large, using sports to expand the church's reach.

Men like Dungy, Brown, and Tebow aren't the genesis of the concerns this marriage has forged, they are the symptoms.

With sports so intertwined with a Christian doctrine that has long marginalized and vilified gay people—hell, their sin allegedly took down the cities of Sodom and Gomorrah—it's easy to understand why gay people might pause before engaging in the world of athletics.

There is an entire Christian doctrine claiming the existence of a sinister class of sins called "abominations." Somehow abominations like homosexuality are worse than your average sin. It's certainly frowned upon to cheat and steal, and to cheat on your wife, but you can recover from that. Some prayer, a request for forgiveness, and the Lord will set you free. But an abomination? That is a whole other level of sin, something from under which one cannot so easily escape.

Murdering your dog or stealing from a department store are your basic, run-of-the-mill sins. Gay sex with your husband? That's a far worse "abomination" to many devout Christians. Go figure.

Interestingly, the line in Leviticus about a man lying with a man is followed by, *They are to be put to death; their blood will be on their own heads.* So why is Dungy not advocating for the mass murder of gay people? The Word of God orders gay people to be put to death. Like all other Christians, Dungy picks and chooses from the Bible what suits him. One clause about abomination fits his worldview and his "brand" of Christianity, so he embraces it; the other clause about killing gay people won't fly in 2015, so he and other Christians find a way to ignore it with claims of a "new covenant" that gives them cover when they need it.

Think that's hyperbole? It isn't. Scott Lively is an author and former candidate for governor of Massachusetts. He took some heat after making the claim that gay sex is worse in God's eyes than killing people. He didn't back down.

*So, is homosexuality worse than mass murder from God's standpoint?* Lively wrote on his blog. *Read it for yourself . . . God Himself employed mass killing to punish sexual perversion. Very harsh in human estimation, but who are we to judge God?*

Certainly many Christians would not say they accept this. Different believers would order the litany of possible sins in many different ways. Yet it's informative to understand just how rooted homophobia and anti-gay discrimination are in the Bible, which Dungy and so many other Christians in sports use to indoctrinate impressionable athletes.

There are other fascinating laws laid out in the Old Testament. It's easy to make a mockery of the Bible with talk of not eating shrimp or a woman laying unclean or killing a goat after giving birth. Heck, the Bible even outlaws tattoos (popular with so many athletes). Football itself—played with a pigskin—is against the rules. These things are right there in the Bible, yet they are magically ignored by people like Dungy. But gay sex remains an abomination.

*Lying lips are abomination to the LORD: but they that deal truly are His delight.*

That's a much-ignored passage in the Book of Proverbs in the King James Bible that calls lying, yes, an "abomination," equal to homosexuality in the lines of God's Bible. One of the Ten Commandments forbids giving "false testimony," a fancy way of saying, *Don't lie.* (Though some interpret it narrowly about testifying in some court of law, many see the broader message "God" seemed to be sending.) Either way, lying is forbidden over and over and over again in the Bible, both in the New and Old Testaments, from the Word of God and Jesus Christ (who, by the way, never mentions homosexuality). It is mentioned far more often than sex between men. Lying is one of the most important actions you simply cannot perform, right there with being paid to play football on Sundays.

So if the Bible is so important to him, why does Tony Dungy lie?

Shortly after the NFL draft, Dungy told the *Tampa Tribune* that he would not have drafted Michael Sam, who had come out publicly as gay just months earlier. "I wouldn't want to deal with all of it," Dungy said. "It's not going to be totally smooth . . . things will happen."

Dungy's history of homophobia goes beyond his verbal and financial endorsement of the IFI's crusade against gay people. As recently as 2013, when Jason Collins came out publicly, Dungy wasn't afraid to say that he didn't "agree" with the gay NBA player's "lifestyle."

The homophobia label was again pasted on Dungy's forehead when he said he wouldn't want Michael Sam on his team. Days later, Dungy released an indignant statement that he felt would clarify his perspective: "The media attention that comes with it will be a distraction. Unfortunately we are all seeing this play out now, and I feel badly that my remarks played a role in the distraction."

The former coach couched his homophobia against Sam here in a concern for his team and the dreaded "distraction." Yet Dungy had no problem being a rare African American head coach in a formerly whites-only profession, which brought questions about his place in history as the first black head coach to win the Super Bowl. Distraction! He has also never shied away from proselytizing, creating media attention for himself and his team based on his religion. Distraction!

Dungy specifically called out the announced Oprah Winfrey–produced documentary as part of the reason he originally said he wouldn't want to draft Michael Sam, due to the distractions it would bring. The problem is, the Oprah show hadn't been announced when Dungy made the comments. Oops!

Dungy wasn't just a liar about his concerns over having Sam on his team, he was a hypocrite too, something Jesus Christ himself called an abomination in the Book of Luke. In 2011, Dungy actively supported the return of dog-murderer Michael Vick back to the NFL even though—wait for it—a documentary film crew was producing a TV show about him at the same time. Dungy was out front in the media telling reporters and TV cameras that he trusted Vick and that the animal-killer wouldn't be a problem.

"When [Vick] kind of described that to me and the fact that he needed to get back closer to the Lord," Dungy said, "that's when I said, *I'm going to stay involved in this. I'm going to help you.*"

When a dog-killing Christian was the focus of intense media scrutiny and the subject of a documentary, Dungy pushed NFL coaches to hire him. When a gay man of undisclosed religious affiliation was the topic, Dungy didn't want him on his team. As long as you're a member of the Conservative Christian Club, you can do no wrong.

"You hypocrite," Jesus said in the Book of Matthew, "first take the plank out of your own eye, and then you will see clearly to remove the speck from your brother's eye."

After video was leaked in September 2014 of Baltimore Ravens running back Ray Rice punching his wife, Dungy came to the player's defense, saying he would absolutely welcome the wife-beater onto his team. "I would have to talk to him and say, *Have you learned from this?*" Dungy said on NBC. "Look in his eye and see if he has learned from his mistake. Then I'd be okay to sign him."

The key here isn't a debate about whether a wife-beater deserves to play in the NFL. The important piece for this conversation is the "media distraction" that signing Rice would cause. The protests it would generate. The scrutiny it would invite.

For Dungy, just as with so many other people who claim to be Christian, being gay is truly worse than killing dogs for fun and beating your wife. It's worse than lying. Being gay, to Dungy, disqualifies someone from playing on his team. The media distraction surrounding killing animals and punching your wife is acceptable; a few cameras asking questions about a gay athlete are not.

Heck, at the time the Bible was written, both killing dogs for fun and beating your wife were perfectly accepted in society, so I guess we should understand the 2,000-year-old thinking of Dungy.

I contacted Dungy to talk with him about all of this. Sadly, he declined to comment.

It's no surprise that when Dungy's son committed suicide just before Christmas in 2005, many wondered aloud if his son had ended his life because he was gay, listening for years to his father's anti-gay mantra. According to the Trevor Project, LGB youth are four times more likely to attempt suicide than their straight peers; on top of that, LGB youth in disapproving families are over eight times more likely to try to kill themselves than are LGB youth in families with no disapproval.

Only Dungy's family knows if there's any truth to this. The implication of the speculation is clear: Dungy's outward rejection of gay people creates a perceived hostile environment wherever he goes, whether it's his own home or the locker room.

\* \* \*

Given the marriage between Christianity and sports in America, it's no wonder that lower levels of sports turn a blind eye to blatant pro-discrimination policies. There is no more powerful place that religion affects LGBT athletes than at Christian high schools and colleges maintaining anti-gay policies. The fact that these schools are allowed to remain in associations like the NCAA and NAIA is a true abomination.

In the spring of 2015, I met a young man at a Christian school in the South who was excited to share his story publicly on *Outsports*. He had grown up Christian in a Southern state and came out to open arms on his high school team. He won a state championship for that team and was beloved at his school. He chose to attend a Christian college so he could earn his degree while getting closer to God. Shortly before starting his freshman year he learned the school has an anti-gay policy and had fired faculty members for being gay. He went back in the closet as he listened to invited speakers his first week on campus tell students that homosexuality was something to be dreaded and hated, not embraced. Regardless, he slowly came back out to select people on his team and eventually got the courage to share his story with the world.

"LGBT athletes need more voices," he told me, "and I believe that my story can help others find their voice and also save lives."

The day before we ran the story, the athlete called me crying. He couldn't go through with it. The school could easily remove his scholarship and kick him out, all because he's gay. His family simply couldn't afford that risk. They had fired faculty for being gay, so the fear was legitimate. Thus, another athlete was pushed back into the closet, unable to share his story and continue the domino effect that has led to so many more young people finding comfort in their own skin. He was simply another victim of anti-gay religious policies.

A closeted gay assistant basketball coach at a Southern Christian school was told by his head coach that he couldn't tell anyone else that he's gay or he would be fired. As I mentioned before, Belmont University fired successful women's soccer coach Lisa Howe after she allegedly announced she and her female partner were having a baby. Yes, this Christian school fired an expecting mother, removing an important source of income to provide for her child.

The Georgia Association of Christian Schools is a conglomeration of high schools based on the adoption of an unbreakable statement of faith that forbids the hiring of any gay teacher or coach.

*We reject any attempt to "reinterpret" Scripture in light of "modern" moral or psychological theories. In the Biblical account of creation, the family was the first societal institution ordained by God. (Genesis 1:27; 2:18-22) Furthermore, Scripture plainly declares that the first two humans created by God were a man and a woman. (Genesis 1:27; 2:18-22) God commanded the man and the woman to be fruitful, multiply, and replenish the earth. (Genesis 1:28) Accordingly, all forms of homosexuality, lesbianism, bisexuality, bestiality, incest, fornication, adultery, and pornography are sinful perversions of God's gift of sex. (Genesis 2:24; 19:5; 13; 26:8-9; Leviticus 18:1-30; Romans 1:26-29; I Corinthians 5:1; 6:9; I Thessalonians 4:1-8; Hebrews 13:4) Since we believe that all sexual activity outside of a marriage between a man and a woman, including homosexual practices, are in direct opposition to God's Word and constitute a direct contradiction to God's institution of the home, we will not retain in membership any school who promotes by their faculty, homosexual behavior or any other sexual activity outside of a Biblical marriage.*

Of course, there is no mention of the sins of eating shrimp or playing football or having a tattoo. Gay people are called out specifically, taking up almost a quarter of the entire statement.

What's particularly sad is the clear double standard applied to gay people. While the statement talks about forgiveness of sin by Jesus Christ, this one particular "sin"—homosexuality—is the only one called out for exclusion from members schools. It is, as I've said, THE abomination of abominations.

While this is the policy of an entire collection of high schools in Georgia, it mirrors policies at NCAA and NAIA member schools across the country. Azusa Pacific University in NCAA Division II fired a trans professor in 2013. Shorter University, also in NCAA Division II, actively banned gay employees in 2011. High-profile schools are not immune. Baylor University banned homosexuality from its campus until 2015, and still has a policy infringing on students' First Amendment right to association: *It is thus expected that Baylor students will not participate in advocacy groups which promote understandings of sexuality that are contrary to biblical teaching.*

All of these schools and many others are allowed to remain in the NCAA and NAIA. Yet on the NCAA's own website it contradicts that policy clearly: *We seek to establish and maintain an inclusive culture that fosters equitable participation for student-athletes and career opportunities for coaches and administrators from diverse backgrounds.*

The Big Ten named one of its highest football honors after Tony Dungy. It wasn't an award for defensive play or coaching, for which Dungy was known on the field. It was the Big Ten Humanitarian Award. One of college football's biggest conferences, and one of the NCAA's highest-profile members, has named its Humanitarian Award after a man who has actively fought against equality for gay people.

The NCAA might as well take its diversity policy and hit the *Delete* button. If the association is going to apply it only to schools that want to sign on, it's not worth the pixels it's printed with.

Truth be told, more and more Christians in sports are returning to the roots of Christianity, shifting away from Tony Dungy and the laws of the Old Testament and focusing more on the love of the New Testament.

"Yes, that's your brother. And you love your brother."

That was the response Michael Irvin's father—a Southern Baptist minister—gave him when Irvin saw his brother one night clad in a dress and high heels. It was the first time Irvin realized his brother was gay or transgender or both. Irvin struggled with his acceptance of his brother for years, knowing the ridicule he could face, from those less understanding, if they knew his brother wore dresses. Yet he kept coming back to those loving words of his father. There is no more stereotypically homophobic person in America than the Southern Baptist minister. Yet Irvin's father put aside the few passages in the Bible about homosexuality and focused on the overwhelming message the New Testament and the words of Jesus Christ.

> *Blessed are the peacemakers, for they will be called sons of God.*
> *Do not judge, or you too will be judged.*

When you're in Michael Irvin's presence, it's immediately clear he approaches life and his faith from that same positive, welcoming perspective. He smiles, he laughs, he hugs, he listens. Why was he a great leader in the Dallas Cowboys' locker room? Not because he could catch the ball. Not because he was Jesus-loving Christian. Not because he could muscle cornerbacks out of the way. It's because he knew how to communicate with people in a way that empowered them, instead of making them feel judged. He welcomed everyone, cast aside no one. It's those men who make great leaders. People with closed hearts and closed minds can be dictators. They can force players to perform; it's certainly one style of leadership. But people who are able to connect with others—with everyone—and value them for who they are, those people are true leaders of human beings.

Of all the interviews I've done with athletes, one of the standouts was quarterback Landry Jones. I met him at the NFLPA Premiere Event in 2013—he had just been drafted out of the University of Oklahoma by the Pittsburgh Steelers.

I get wary every time I approach a pro athlete to talk about LGBT issues, whether it's same-sex marriage or just having a teammate who's gay.

As I've mentioned, an executive with the NFLPA talked to me about my questions before I interviewed Jones. I was told that I had to get the permission of the players before asking any questions. I played ball, and a couple of them declined.

I almost didn't approach Jones—as he walked around I noticed he had written a passage from the Book of Philippians on his hand. I hadn't seen that before. Even Tebow had just put a verse number on his eye black; Jones actually wrote out the verse on his hand. My own fear of Christians in that moment made me turn away from him, assuming a rejection. Thankfully I caught myself, turned back, and fired away. He agreed to talk with me, and I immediately asked him about the verse on his hand and the idea that Christians and the LGBT community are in conflict.

"There's not a conflict," Jones said. "People are people and God tells us to love everybody. And so that's what I do."

When he said the words, they felt like a canned line strung together by a handler who'd trained him to "say the right thing." But as he talked more, it became clear that this young man was opening his heart and mind to me on an issue he felt surprisingly comfortable talking about.

"Now, do I condone what they're doing? No, I don't think it's right," he continued. I could feel the NFLPA folks over my shoulder anticipating the media firestorm that would envelop Jones once his comments got out.

Except, he took a turn I wasn't expecting.

"But, am I going to go out there and not talk to them? Am I going to go out there and be hateful and mean to them? I think that's ignorant. I think we respect and love everybody. But there's also a moral standard there for me, and I'm going to take a stand on that. I don't think it's right, but it's their life and I'm not going to go up because someone is gay and be mean or hateful and say terrible things to them. I'm going to treat them like a human being."

It is exceedingly difficult to convince some devout Christians—born Christian, taught Christianity, who value Christ above everything else in their lives—that gay sex isn't a sin. On the flip side, it's equally tough to convince some gay people—part of whose identity is based on gay sex and who have been persecuted for it—that Christians don't, because of that entrenched belief, represent a danger to their community.

Sports are the ultimate equalizer. The basketball hoop doesn't care if you're gay. The pigskin doesn't care if you believe in Jesus. After the first tip-off of a game, all of the issues society spends so much time debating don't matter a damn. That dynamic of athletics has been its greatest contribution to society, and it has made every sport—particularly team sports—the ultimate tool to integrate society.

"It doesn't matter if you're gay or if you're straight," Jones said to me. "If you can play the game of football, you're going to be on a team and you're going to have a job. Just like if you're in a regular business setting. If you can do your job well, you can do your job. You can get paid and earn a living and provide for your family, whatever your family looks like."

*Whatever your family looks like.* This is a deeply Christian man. He had written a Bible verse on his hand, and not a famous one like John 3:16, but one from the freaking Book of Philippians.

There will be people like Dungy, who focus on hateful doctrine, for eternity. Yet their power is in the rearview mirror. Landry Jones, Michael Irvin—they are the path forward.

# Michael Irvin Demonstrates the Role of Straight Athletes in a Gay Movement

**Michael Irvin didn't hesitate** when I invited him to do a cover story for the "Sports Issue" of *Out* magazine in 2011. *Out* is the most-read gay men's magazine in the country whose cover often features straight people like Johnny Knoxville, Andy Samberg, and Britney Spears. The editorial staff wanted to demonstrate how far sports had come in accepting gay people. In 2011, with so few prominent gay athletes, highlighting our straight "allies" was just about the only way to get a big name on the cover. Never before had a straight professional athlete been on the magazine's cover.

I'd met Irvin several years earlier when his then–radio cohost Kevin Kiley asked me to come on their weekly show to analyze some NFL games. Imagine that: me, some gay sports writer, breaking down games for a Hall of Famer and three-time Super Bowl champ. Irvin had his doubts as well—why on earth did he need some gay guy talking NFL matchups? But when I spent two minutes breaking down the Chiefs-Patriots game in Week 1 of the 2008 season, he was a bit stunned.

"Hold up, hold up," Irvin said, interrupting a rant I was on about the Cowboys. "Now just wait one minute."

Michael has this "cat that ate the canary" laugh that rolls out of him when he's come to an epiphany. It's as though he's laughing at himself for not seeing it before. It's one of his trademarks, something you notice after spending some quality time with him.

"That was good stuff," he said. "You broke those games down like a pro, Cyd. That was as good a job as anyone."

"What did you expect," I asked, "a bunch of tight end jokes?"

That sealed the deal. It's exactly what he had been thinking, and I called him on it in a fun, disarming way. They invited me to come back the next week and analyze some more games. Irvin was hooked.

I appeared on his show in Dallas and Miami for the next three years. We developed a bit of a friendship—Michael seemed to trust me. So when I asked him to do the cover story for *Out*, he went all in.

"If we're gonna do this," he said, "we're gonna do it right."

"Yeah, sure, no problem. You know I'll treat you right—"

"No, Cyd," he cut in. "If we're gonna do this, I'm gonna tell you everything. We're gonna get people talking about this. We're gonna start a national conversation. It's time we talked about my brother."

His older brother Vaughn had been either transgender or a drag queen (Michael isn't sure), as Michael discovered one night on a drive home with his father, when they spotted Vaughn leaving the house in a dress and high heels. It was something Michael had never talked about, not with his pastor TD Jakes, not with his Cowboys teammates, not with the media. The only time he mentioned it before was in passing during an interview with me on his radio show in that 2008 season. I caught it but let it go. I'd circle back when the time was right.

It was something Michael had wrestled with for years, his only guidance coming from his Southern Baptist father: "Yes, that's your brother. And you love your brother."

In a series of interviews over the couple of weeks after his decision to do the cover story, Michael opened up with me for the first time about not just his brother but issues of the day like having a gay teammate and same-sex marriage.

Meanwhile, the internal debate at the magazine was about whether to put Irvin on the cover. While I had told Michael he'd be on the cover, it had yet to be decided. It would depend on what images were gleaned from the photo shoot: the editor wanted a shirtless shot and I wanted nothing to do with that. What the editorial staff didn't seem to understand was that Michael was a Hall of Fame NFL player, one of the greatest of all time. And he was a ladies' man—infamously so. You don't just ask the guy known simply as "The Playmaker" to whip off his shirt for the gays.

When Michael got to the shoot location—a nook tucked away behind some rundown storefronts on Hollywood Boulevard—I intercepted him. He gave me a big hug and, as we walked toward wardrobe, I told him he should only do what he's comfortable doing.

It was as though he already had a game plan for that photo shoot mapped out by Norv Turner and vetted by Jimmy Johnson. It took no time to get him into wardrobe and stripped down to his black boxer briefs, like he'd mentally prepared for what a "gay" photo shoot might look like.

With the stylist, Michael picked out some cargo pants and boots. They were masculine and stylish. The big question was what to wear as a shirt. That's when Michael spied an old set of leather shoulder pads and a helmet the likes of which George Halas and Red Grange donned in their storied careers. Michael gawked, slipped on the shoulder pads, plopped the helmet on his head, and looked in the mirror. No shirt, just the shoulder pads.

"Now that's hot," he said.

He was right. A lot of guys let their bodies go after they retire. Not Michael. In his forties, Michael looked as though he'd never stopped playing. Known during his career for his strength, his biceps were still popping out of his skin, his abs still defined.

It was the cover shot I knew could elevate the conversation about gay men in football. As was previously discussed, so often the hang-up is the locker room: gay guys getting naked with straight guys. If a man's man like Michael Irvin takes off his clothes and appears shirtless in a gay men's magazine, it could send a message just as strong as the words I would lay out on the page. And ultimately, it would have all been his idea, his choice.

As Michael marched toward the set, I caught his eye with a raised brow. "You good with this?" I asked.

"Let's go cause a shitstorm," he laughed, striding out the door.

For the next hour he posed and smiled like it was a photo shoot for a car company or sports drink. He was in his element. At one point he looked down at the pants, surveyed the waistline, and pulled them down farther to reveal more of his underwear— Calvins, if you must know. Every move he made with that wardrobe was his to make, and it was brilliant.

This, we both knew, was a game-changer.

When the story hit the newsstands it was on *SportsCenter* and plastered across the web. Michael got countless texts and phone calls about it from friends in the league. Some asked why he did it. Others thanked him—it was a conversation too long in coming.

Michael agreed to only one interview in the days following the magazine's release—for his employer, the NFL Network. They brought him to LA to talk about why he did the article, why he finally opened up about his brother. He nailed it: "When we start talking about equality, I'm an African American, so you know what should reign in all of our hearts when it comes to equality. Equality for all means equality for all. So when we start talking about being on the magazine, the more we talk about things, and the more we talk about them in a calm way, the better we are as a country. I get guys, and even when I step in here, Warren [Sapp] and all the guys, *What, why you gotta toot up your lips in the picture?* and all of that stuff. But the reality is, it gets us talking about something that's very serious, and that's equality for everybody."

*Bam.*

After that NFL interview, Irvin did something truly amazing, particularly for him: He shut up. He got out of the way. GLAAD wanted him to show up at one of their functions to accept an award; he declined. Other media outlets asked him to share his thoughts with them; he said no. It wasn't because he wanted to run away from the issue—he had very consciously and very strategically embraced it.

Instead, he inherently understood the role of an ally. While Irvin was known for seeking out the limelight as a player, the roles were reversed here. He wasn't the guy running with the ball, he was the downfield receiver laying the blocks for Emmitt Smith. Maybe it's because he's African American that this came second-nature to him, or maybe it's because he was raised in poverty. Either way, Michael knew his role as a straight man on gay issues was to open opportunities for conversation, then let other people—gay people—do the talking. He knew he had to do everything in his power—including taking off his shirt and showing off his Calvins—to elevate the conversation. Mission accomplished. He'd continue the chatter on his weekly radio show, but the spotlight on this issue was not his to take—he was not the affected party.

It's a lesson many other "straight allies" have followed since. Scott Fujita, the former Saints and Browns linebacker and NFLPA rep, didn't shy away from sharing his supportive views on same-sex marriage and gay teammates when he was with the New Orleans Saints. Whether it was conversations in the locker room or an interview with *Outsports*, Fujita lent his voice where it needed to be. Yet as LGBT spokespeople in sports—like Conner Mertens, Jason Collins, and even Jim Buzinski and myself—elevated their public profiles, Fujita quickly and naturally stepped into the background.

A week before Michael Sam came out, former Saints linebacker Jonathan Vilma told NFL Network that he did not want a gay teammate because the guy might look at him in the showers. It wasn't the first time Vilma had dipped his toe into the subject, saying previously that men should not have "female tendencies" and then refusing to talk about what he meant. (When I asked him about it on Twitter, he blocked me.)

My first post-Vilma-comment text message was to Fujita. The two had been teammates on the Super Bowl champion New Orleans Saints, and they had engaged on gay issues in the locker room in the past. Fujita quietly connected with Vilma and the two engaged privately on the topic of gay teammates. A week later, after Sam's coming-out, Vilma's perspective shifted slightly, and his public comments changed.

"The point I was trying to make, or the context I was trying to take it in, is that I've never been put in that situation. No player in the NFL has been put in that situation. So it's not as simple as anyone saying, *Well, there's nothing wrong with it,*" Vilma told Anderson Cooper on CNN. "I don't see anything wrong with it. You have other players that may, you have other players that may not."

Fujita wasn't interested in talking publicly or getting in front of a camera. He was focused on having impactful conversations with Vilma and me behind the scenes and finding a way to build bridges. That has been Fujita's MO on this subject for years. He even talked to Vilma about chatting with me, but it didn't pan out; though I doubt Vilma remembered blocking me from Twitter two years earlier.

Many in the gay community have clamored for these straight

men to be more outspoken, to get on TV and fight the good fight publicly. So many gay people seek out public validation in the form of open conversation; they get it when news items arise or when these athletes are asked a question by a reporter. Yet far too many LGBT activists mistake talking heads for doing real work.

These athletes know better. They lend their voices when and where it is needed—select opportunities where the voice of a powerful straight "ally" could elevate the conversation. While guys like Irvin and Fujita were declining the interviews, they were still fighting. Behind the scenes, they were having conversations and opening opportunities. These men weren't interested in grabbing the spotlight on this issue.

In 2012, three straight men emerged in sports and became the darlings of the sports media. At a time when sports writers seemed uninterested in talking with actual LGBT athletes, the sudden enhanced celebrity of these three men elevated the public discussion of these issues in sports like never before. It also opened a conversation within the LGBT sports movement about whether straight people could go "too far" in becoming the faces of a movement, drawing attention away from the affected LGBT athletes and activists.

Imagine a white man becoming the face of the civil rights movement in the 1960s. Robert Kennedy, for example, decides he's going to talk more in the media about race, he's going to go on the campaign trail through the universities of the Northeast collecting high speakers fees to preach to the choir on the issue. He becomes the darling of the New York elite, the white man helping the affected blacks. Instead of Martin Luther King Jr. becoming the first African American named *Time*'s Person of the Year in 1963, Kennedy snags the honor two years after his brother. It's

November 20—Kennedy's birthday—that we recognize every year to mark the civil rights movement, not January 15.

Or imagine a man being the face of the fight for women's reproductive rights. In this scenario, Supreme Court Justice Harry Blackmun casts aside Jane Roe (her real name was Norma Leah McCorvey) and steps down from the court to claim victory for liberty and appear on Sunday-morning talk shows to discuss gender equality.

To be sure, RFK and Blackmun had indelible marks on the social-justice movements to which their actions contributed. Racial and gender equality would not be where they are today if not for these two white men. The same could be said for three other cisgender straight men—Hudson Taylor, Chris Kluwe, and Brendon Ayanbadejo—each of whom stormed the conversation about LGBT equality in sports in 2012, helping pull attention to the issues at a crucial historical moment.

When then–University of Maryland wrestler Hudson Taylor placed an LGBT-supportive sticker on his helmet, we at *Outsports* noticed. Jim wrote glowingly of the athlete's support for the community. We became big fans of Taylor as he spoke at universities about standing up for the disenfranchised LGBT community. He even created Athlete Ally, an organization to mobilize straight athletes to fight for LGBT equality in sports.

He was quickly cast as a face of the LGBT sports movement, not simply a supporter of it. He had the backing of some deep-pocketed people in New York City, Washington, DC, and across the country set on making him the great hero of the movement. His organization quickly amassed a six-figure budget and would dominate media conversations when stories broke.

Two NFL players also rose to prominence in the national conversation. Both Ravens linebacker Brendon Ayanbadejo and Vikings punter Chris Kluwe were instrumental in bringing awareness to marriage-equality measures in Minnesota and Maryland in 2012. When a Maryland elected official wrote a letter to Ayanbadejo's coach telling him to stop his player from supporting same-sex marriage rights, Kluwe penned an awesome response for *Deadspin* that ignited the conversation about the issues across the sports world.

*I can assure you that gay people getting married will have zero effect on your life*, Kluwe wrote. *They won't come into your house and steal your children. They won't magically turn you into a lustful cockmonster. They won't even overthrow the government in an orgy of hedonistic debauchery because all of a sudden they have the same legal rights as the other 90 percent of our population . . .*

He was, of course, completely correct. The style with which he delivered that completely correct information put the message front-and-center in the sports world and elevated the entire cause. It was brilliant.

All three of these men—Taylor, Kluwe, and Ayanbadejo—elevated the struggle immensely. They wanted to make the sports world—heck, the whole world—a better place for LGBT people. Each of them spent time and energy working with LGBT athletes and straight people trying to build bridges and bring equality to sports and beyond. The national conversation would not be where it is today without the chaos Kluwe and Ayanbadejo caused in 2012. The elite gay establishment would not have embraced sports as quickly as it did if not for Taylor. These men left important marks on the LGBT sports movement, and for that I am very grateful.

And.

Along the way, a rift developed between these three straight men and part of the LGBT community, including myself, because lesbian activists and gay athletes believed these men were (sometimes unintentionally) taking opportunities away from LGBT people looking to share their own stories. The complaint wasn't without merit—I know of at least two instances when Taylor and Ayanbadejo (probably unknowingly) accepted appearance invitations that likely would have gone to an LGBT person. That confused the role of the "ally" in the minds of many; while we cannot achieve equality without true allies, we also knew it was futile to fight for equality without lifting the voices of LGBT people in sports. It was a catch-22.

These weren't bad men. They were trying to help, and they *were* helping. Yet it seemed they got caught at a critical turning point in the LGBT sports movement—between a time practically void of LGBT people able to speak on the issues and a burgeoning "new era" when there were more of them than any camera could cover.

An internal fight ensued, with some in the movement rejecting Taylor for his seeming refusal to highlight more LGBT voices, even as so many LGBT people outside of sports embraced him, not knowing what transpired behind the scenes.

In 2013, Ayanbadejo stumbled when he told a reporter for the *Baltimore Sun* that four gay pro athletes might be talking about coming out together at the same time. It created a media frenzy that led to a gay-football witch hunt of sorts. When he had the opportunity to walk back his comments with Anderson Cooper, he reiterated that he and various organizations and individuals knew of different athletes thinking about coming out.

"And potentially it's possible, it's fathomable, that they could possibly do something together and break a story together."

Potentially it's possible and fathomable that they could possibly do something? Ugh. Ayanbadejo stepped back from the spotlight after that episode; he had learned a valuable lesson.

Kluwe stepped back a bit following his kerfuffle with the Minnesota Vikings. After a year of claiming he may have been released by the team due to his support of same-sex marriage, a report was issued that suggested that while Kluwe probably heard some bad things, he may have been cut because the Vikings could get a younger replacement with about equal production for $1 million less.

Kluwe went all-in, claiming the report didn't reflect the entire investigation. What had been a fight about LGBT equality in sports seemed to become overshadowed by a pissing contest between the Vikings and their disgruntled former employee. He brought the National Center for Lesbian Rights into his corner, and the episode ended well for Kluwe, and very well for the LGBT people for whom he fought, with the Vikings committing to further sensitivity trainings (they had already engaged in some) and donations to several key LGBT groups. Like Ayanbadejo, Kluwe then faded into the background of the movement, content with having brought so much attention and money to the cause.

I have a special place in my heart for Ayanbadejo and Kluwe. They were both invited to a special dinner at my good friend Howard Bragman's house the night before Michael Sam came out publicly. I have appeared alongside them in the media and at other public functions. These two men quickly came to understand the role of a true ally in a social-justice movement. I have tons of respect for them both.

Regardless of the internal debates of that movement, all three of these men helped move the needle at a time when we desperately needed a spark. In 2012, the sports media were still uninterested in talking with LGBT athletes about their perspectives. These three men in particular filled a void at a critical time.

Taylor, Kluwe, and Ayanbadejo, along with several others like rugby player Ben Cohen, helped ramp up the movement to end homophobia in sports in an important way. They were the bridge between a time when articulate LGBT people in sports were hard to find and the current day when we are everywhere.

To understand how to be the perfect ally, we just need to examine the actions of one man. Branch Rickey was the white general manager and president of the Brooklyn Dodgers who decided in the mid-1940s that he would integrate baseball. He understood it wouldn't do any good for him to pound his fist and make proclamations to the media about the need for acceptance. The only way for Rickey to build acceptance of African Americans in pro sports—and society in general—was to elevate black athletes.

Jackie Robinson became the face of Rickey's integration efforts. Having a black man in the locker room and on the field opened the eyes of fans, players, and management in a way no white man talking about racism ever could. Some people rejected Robinson. Others embraced him. While Rickey could do some of the talking, no one could walk that walk other than a black person. Young African American kids suddenly had someone to look up to, someone to aspire to be. Robinson's example helped create an entire generation of black athletes who saw the sky as the limit. That wasn't reality before 1947.

No white man could have ever done that, just as no straight man could ever do what Michael Sam and Jason Collins have done for so many gay kids playing sports today.

Now, just like African American athletes today, LGBT people in sports are taking the mantle that was always theirs. They can speak for themselves on the issues. They can fight for themselves. More and more they are playing openly. Yet with the NFL's collective wariness of Michael Sam, the need for true, powerful allies like Rickey is still evident.

Patrick Burke didn't care much about LGBT rights or gay athletes seven years ago. There was good reason: the Philadelphia Flyers scout had battled severe depression for years—many days just getting out of bed was a challenge. He had other struggles to cope with and other issues more near and dear to him and his family.

Even when his brother, Miami (Ohio) University hockey team student manager Brendan Burke, came out publicly in a story on ESPN in late 2009, LGBT issues were going to be his brother's fight. Patrick would be there to support Brendan when he needed it, but changing the face of hockey for LGBT people would take someone in the community like his brother.

On February 5, 2010, that all changed when Brendan died in a car crash on an icy Indiana road. A month later I saw Patrick at the GLAAD Awards. "I don't know what I'm going to do," he told me that night, "but I'm going to do something."

While he had planned to just be the backup support for his brother's efforts, Patrick suddenly cast himself as the warrior, creating the You Can Play project to highlight those people—gay and straight—who welcomed anyone onto their team as long as they could shoot the ball or catch passes.

The slogan of the project was simple: *Gay athletes. Straight allies. Teaming up for respect.* To be sure, Patrick did not shy away from the media. He built a powerful following on social media and was television gold when the cameras were rolling. He accepted some speaking engagements, but only as the facilitator of conversations between LGBT people in sports.

Patrick ran You Can Play for the first two years. Recognizing that the movement needed more 1) gay people, and 2) racial minorities at the forefront, he tapped gay former NFL prospect Wade Davis to replace him as executive director. Patrick then drifted into the background, having created an entire platform for Davis to use as a megaphone.

Like Irvin and Rickey before him, Patrick inherently understood the quintessential role of an ally.

(Frankly, I don't really like the term "ally." It's like a gold star that people give themselves. When earned, it's just code for "decent human being." I don't need a gold star for doing what's right to help people who aren't like me. I reject the label of "ally" when someone places it on me; it's enough for me to know I'm helping somebody else.)

There's a truth that is at the heart of social change across LGBT issues: straight people don't change minds on the acceptance of gay people nearly as regularly or effectively as the voices and visibility of gay people themselves, together with their trans brothers and sisters.

Dick Cheney publicly supported same-sex marriage rights before Barack Obama. Think about that. The man cast as Darth Vader by many gay people actually supported gay rights earlier than almost any prominent Democrat. Why? It certainly wasn't because of afternoon teas with Nancy Pelosi telling him he had to be open-minded. The reason was simple: his daughter is gay. Period.

My father's attitudes about gay people didn't change because of the influence of his friends, or because a straight news anchor on CBS educated him about gay people. He changed because his son came out as gay.

While it's a Disney movie, *Remember the Titans* is built on the same premise. The white coaches could yell at their athletes to respect their black teammates all they wanted; but it wasn't until the black athletes showed up, lived with the white athletes, and performed on the field that respect developed.

You can't train or lecture someone into accepting people of another race or sexual orientation; in so many cases, only members of the affected group can change hearts and minds.

It's a truth that the LGBT sports movement understood years ago. Having the support of straight people is essential to change. Most gay athletes don't get the opportunity to play unless a straight coach gives it to them. Most gay athletes are surrounded by straight teammates who must accept them. The people in the NFL and the NFLPA who included sexual orientation protection in the 2011 collective bargaining agreement—most, if not all of them, are straight. Sports are dominated by the power of straight people, and straight men in particular.

Yet to reach those straight athletes and coaches who are far from allies, you need LGBT people. Some of them grew up with a minister condemning homosexuality and never really got to know any gay people. Others find homosexuality to be an affront to their masculine self-identity. They define their masculinity and their heterosexuality in part by participating in only the toughest of sports—a gay man in the locker next to them dismantles their very identity.

Straight teammates usually can't reach those people very effectively by preaching support. Straight activists talking about the need to welcome gay teammates doesn't often hit home. It takes people like Michael Sam sharing the torment he felt living in the closet to get at the hearts and minds of the people who most need to hear those stories.

LGBT people sharing their personal stories is the key to social change.

The day after Michael Sam was cut by the St. Louis Rams in August 2014, he was not picked up by another NFL team. While Sam's drop in the draft down to pick number 249 was an early warning that NFL teams didn't want a publicly out gay player on their team, Sam sitting at home while other players were being scooped up was deeply problematic.

I had spent a lot of time and energy defending the NFL as a meritocracy where Sam's sexual orientation would not play a factor in his ability to make it in the NFL. That was now crashing down as quite the opposite became more and more apparent. Sam's agents were dumbfounded. I was dumbfounded. Patrick Burke, who had assured me twenty-four hours earlier that Sam would be on the Rams' practice squad, was suddenly left flat-footed.

While there were certainly teams who didn't need him (like the Rams) or whose scheme he didn't fit well (like the Packers), it was time to hit back at the team front offices. I had scheduled an appearance on NFL Network for the next morning and began writing a column about the league's collective failure to find an opportunity for Sam. But I knew this wasn't going to be enough to create any sort of real change.

So I texted Michael Irvin about it. He called me ten minutes later.

Irvin was as perplexed as the rest of us. He'd watched Sam's preseason performance and classified it as anywhere from adequate to impressive. He struggled to find a reason for the NFL's collective lack of interest in him if not his sexual orientation. After I got on NFL Network the next morning and blasted the league, Irvin intended to talk about it publicly on the network's Tuesday preseason show. It had to be addressed.

"How could the Cowboys not call him?" I asked Irvin. Dallas' defense the year before had been bad at an historic level, and their pass defense needed a ton of work. I had already publicly questioned not just why the Cowboys hadn't signed him after his Rams release, but why they hadn't drafted him in the first place.

"I've already talked to Jerry about it," Irvin told me.

Less than forty-eight hours later, the Cowboys signed Sam to their practice squad. Management had run the idea by a few players, all of whom reportedly had no issue with welcoming Sam onto the team. The Jones boys had saved the NFL from a major public relations disaster.

I still don't know how much Irvin had to do with the Cowboys' signing of Sam. I probably never will. But my hunch is that Irvin was again the perfectly powerful straight ally when a gay athlete desperately needed his help, working behind the scenes to open doors for others.

Sam earned an opportunity to participate in the NFL, and people like Dallas Cowboys owner Jerry Jones, St. Louis Rams general manager Les Snead, and Rams head coach Jeff Fisher have been willing and able to crack the door open for him. Sadly, Sam didn't get another opportunity that season, as the Cowboys cut him in October and he wasn't picked up in 2014 or 2015. While it will take athletes like Sam to stand up and be recognized for their true identities, it just might take another Branch Rickey to make sure the doors of opportunity are wide open for gay pro athletes to walk through.

## The Big Lie of the Big Five

***Several years ago I was contacted*** by a member of an NFL cheerleading squad about coming out publicly. She was excited to advance the conversation about LGBT issues in sports, particularly given the lack of out voices in the NFL: Michael Sam hadn't yet revealed his secret to the world. The opportunity to advance the conversation through her was another step, even if it didn't bring an out gay man into the NFL locker room of lore. It wasn't the giant leap we had been so desperately seeking, but it would be another small step.

Female cheerleaders are the darlings of men's sports teams for one main purpose: sexual titillation for the mostly male crowd. These NFL cheerleaders exhibit so many more qualities: athleticism, endurance, charisma, and often—despite the stereotype—intellect. Yet the marketing departments of professional sports teams hire them to attract the attention of straight men with their beautiful faces, perfectly shaped butts, and large breasts.

To have a lesbian come out in that role would generate headlines and turn heads. Frankly, it could titillate some straight men even more. Either way, the conversation about gay people in the NFL would be advanced, even if it was by a woman whose uniform was next to nothing.

The cheerleader's contract with her team didn't allow her to speak to the press without the explicit consent of the team. So she reached out to the team's marketing department asking for permission to come out publicly.

Crickets.

For months the team sat on her request to do an interview with me. The season came and went.

When spring rolled around it was time for cheerleader tryouts— she was selected again. As the following season approached, fear had taken hold again. When Sam came out publicly, as previously discussed, the overwhelming message being sent by people in and out of the NFL was the "distraction" he and any other gay player would bring to a team. The team's lack of response to the cheerleader's request to come out the year before had reinforced the chilling message, intended or not: *Don't rock the boat.*

So she didn't. She lost nerve and interest. Her story was never told. An opportunity was missed. The team's marketing department had ignored the story into oblivion.

It begs the question—why would the team not actively embrace and support a positive story about a gay person finding her truth? We hear inclusive statements from people in sports, and in particular the NFL, all the time, ranging from bench players to coaches to owners to the league commissioner, Roger Goodell. They all say the right things. Green Bay Packers head coach Mike McCarthy, for example, said he would welcome Michael Sam. "Any player who can come here and be a good teammate and follow the rules of our program—which is one, be respectful and produce on the football field—we have room for that guy," he told the *Green Bay Press-Gazette* shortly before Sam's Scouting Combine workout. Sounds wonderful, right? *Come on in, we welcome anybody*, seemed to be the public-facing message.

Except . . .

"Anything that deters from that or detracts from that is not what we're going to be about," Baltimore Ravens head coach John

Harbaugh said at the time while praising Sam. That same caveat was echoed by many coaches and front-office executives.

The men who run professional sports teams don't want anything that isn't "football" near their teams. *Become part of a team* means you learn the Xs and Os, you bring just enough of your personal life into the locker room so the other guys feel like they know you, and everything else gets checked at the stadium gate. Christianity is embraced—and at times used to motivate athletes—but things outside the norm just don't help a team win.

For marketing purposes, these front offices tolerate partnerships with the United Way and the Boys and Girls Clubs. They racially integrated their teams only when their hands were forced by a few forward-thinking men like Branch Rickey (and make no mistake—many of them fought integration until they just couldn't win anymore). Yet most of these men try to steer clear of social issues and politics that make a lot of sports suits uncomfortable. If professional sports leagues had their way, they would exist in a vacuum of hoops and hockey sticks, bats and balls. Conversations about gender and sexual orientation would be kept far away from their courts and fields.

That's the dynamic many of the leagues, teams, and athletes attempt to set up for themselves. Michael Jordan was the most famous example—an elite athlete of elite athletes who kept social and political issues at arm's length. He weathered the occasional criticism for not speaking out, keeping his basketball career completely compartmentalized from society and the cultural issues it faced.

Yet there are some powerful examples to the contrary, like New England Patriots owner Robert Kraft. When same-sex marriage was being argued before the Supreme Court, Kraft instructed the Patriots to sign onto an amicus brief in support of marriage equality. While the Patriots were joined by the San Francisco Giants and

Tampa Bay Rays, no other team or league in professional sports signed on. When the Supreme Court legalized marriage equality for gay people in June 2015, Major League Soccer shared various rainbow-inspired tweets; on the same day, the NFL didn't tweet a thing about the incredible social-justice development while finding time to send messages about the NBA draft, women's soccer, celebrity fans, and the Heisman voting later that year (despite the college football season not yet having begun). The NHL? Nothing. Major League Baseball found time to tweet about a gnome but not about the most significant civil rights decision of the year. The NBA? Nothing (though they did retweet a message about the Warriors at the San Francisco Pride parade two days later).

Professional sports teams are first, second, and third about winning games and winning over fans. Anything that could possibly, conceivably, maybe take away from that must be avoided at all costs. Controversy? Absolutely not. (And to be clear, they view equality like same sex-marriage as controversial.)

That's the big lie of the Big Five sports leagues—that there should be some wall around the stadiums and locker rooms designed to keep out "distractions" like gay athletes or discussions about politics and religion. The leadership of these teams and leagues is so fragile that they fear any minor shift in focus can derail a team's season or disenfranchise a group of fans. Embrace same-sex marriage as an organization? We might lose bigoted fans! Allow a gay player in the locker room? Our homophobic running back might fumble the ball out of fear!

If a couple cheerleaders come out as gay, the season could be over.

How big of a lie is the distraction myth?

The New England Patriots started the 2007 season with a big win over the New York Jets and former Patriots assistant coach

Eric Mangini. The team had high hopes after losing in the AFC Championship game the season before. They had brought in wide receivers Randy Moss and Wes Welker to build what they hoped would be a dominant offense to balance their powerful defense. Some pundits were talking about a "perfect season" before week one; moments after the Patriots clobbered the rival Jets in their opening salvo, 38–14, speculation ran rampant that this team had the potential to be one of the greatest of all time.

The next day, Mangini and his coaching staff accused Patriots coach Bill Belichick of knowingly and illegally videotaping his team's defensive signals. The fallout was widespread and harsh. For the next week, the Patriots were embroiled in one of the hottest midseason controversies in NFL history. Media, fans, and personalities across the league blasted the team and its leadership, creating nicknames like the "Cheatriots" and "Belicheat." The franchise's three previous Super Bowl titles were called into question. Belichick was fined a half-million dollars, the Patriots were fined a quarter-million dollars, and the team lost its first-round pick in the 2008 NFL draft. Thoughts of a perfect season were suddenly thrown out the window: no team could survive the "distraction" of Spygate that would haunt the halls in Foxboro for the rest of the season.

How did the Patriots respond? Days later, in prime time, they crushed the San Diego Chargers—the AFC's best team the previous season—on Sunday Night Football, 38–14. The game was a complete dismantling of one of the NFL's best teams, as the Chargers would advance to the AFC Championship later that season. The Patriots ran off seventeen straight victories after the "distraction," becoming the first team to start an NFL season with an 18–0 record. When the team lost to the New York Giants in the Super Bowl, any "distraction" provided by Spygate was in the distant past.

Seven years later the Patriots were again the subject of a "cheating" scandal when allegations of tampering with the inflation of footballs surfaced days before the 2015 Super Bowl. Media attention and fan criticism swirled around them. While team brass tried to focus the nation's attention on the impending big game, there was no getting away from the hubbub.

How did the Patriots respond? Somehow during the media sessions in the week before the Super Bowl, when the odd question came about Deflategate, the Patriots players brushed it off. That Sunday the Patriots posted the largest second-half comeback in Super Bowl history and stunned the Seattle Seahawks with a last-minute victory.

That same season the Baltimore Ravens were the center of the Ray Rice domestic-violence controversy. Videotape of Rice punching his wife unconscious surfaced the day after their first game of the season and just three days before their Thursday-night face-off against their rival Pittsburgh Steelers. The Ravens were without their star running back and couldn't get away from the domestic-violence controversy that embroiled him.

The Ravens responded by destroying the Steelers 26–6 that week. They made the playoffs, beating the Steelers on the road in their first game and losing a squeaker to the eventual Super Bowl champion Patriots in the divisional round.

In the spring of 2014, the Los Angeles Clippers were the center of a firestorm when tapes were released of owner Donald Sterling using racist language, including some comments targeted at Los Angeles sports hero Magic Johnson. The NBA banned Sterling from the league, and ownership of the team was suddenly up in the air.

How did the Clippers respond? They beat the Golden State Warriors in their playoff series.

Days before USC football's 2014 season opener against

Fresno State, star cornerback Josh Shaw was labeled a "hero" for jumping from a second-story balcony to save his nephew, who was drowning in a pool. He sprained both ankles and was sidelined for weeks.

Except . . . that's not how he sprained his ankles. He didn't save anyone. When the media uncovered the story, Shaw admitted he had jumped from a balcony to avoid police after an argument with his girlfriend. The USC football team got caught up in a torrent of distracting media questions, made worse when a player quit the team and accused head coach Steve Sarkisian of being racist.

Days later, in Sarkisian's debut as USC head coach, the Trojans beat Fresno State 52–13, racking up 702 yards of offense. They finished the season 9–4, ranked in the Top 25 in both the AP and coaches polls.

Green Bay Packers quarterback Brett Favre's father died four days before Christmas in 2003. The next day, a distraught and distracted Favre led his team into Oakland for a game against the Raiders who, despite struggles, had a winning home record. At 8–6 the Packers had struggles of their own, trying to keep pace with the Minnesota Vikings for the NFC North crown. Despite his father's death, Favre put on one of the most flawless displays of his career, throwing for four touchdowns and 399 yards—just three yards shy of his career high at the time—on Monday Night Football. His 311 first-half yards were the most in the NFL in over two seasons. That night he moved into second place all-time for NFL touchdown passes. The Packers beat the Raiders 41–7.

Shortly before their quarterfinal game of the 2014 Division I NCAA football playoffs, North Dakota State players learned their coach was leaving the program to coach the Wyoming Cowboys. Despite various questions swirling around the team, the Bisons won that game and went on to win the national championship.

"We have a focused group of guys who are trying to accomplish greatness," NDSU quarterback Brock Jensen told the *Minneapolis Star-Tribune* after the team's quarterfinal victory. "The world would have to end to affect this team's focus."

The "distraction" myth is the most destructive lie the sports world tells us about gay athletes.

For the most part, the media buys into, and happily perpetuates, this myth. People from beat writers to some of the most respected sports columnists in America give the big leagues cover to avoid truly addressing—and fixing—LGBT issues, along with other social issues.

"Will all the distractions—the network news trucks, the questioning of his teammates about accepting a gay teammate—be worth it?" Peter King wrote for *Sports Illustrated* the day Michael Sam came out publicly.

"If he gets on that team and he doesn't make those plays, then does that become a distraction?" ESPN's Jemele Hill asked.

There is little critical thinking about the Big Five's big lie from most members of the sports media. There is widespread adoption of this idea that a few extra cameras and a couple questions about a gay athlete is reason enough to avoid drafting a Michael Sam altogether. The "distraction" of some media attention is just too powerful a force to expect pro sports brass to make socially conscientious personnel decisions. At least, that's what the sports media echoes.

All of these elite members of the sports media made it perfectly okay for team executives and coaches to say, "No, it's not worth bringing in Sam." They gave cover to bigots who just didn't want to deal with a gay player. All they had to do was talk about the "distraction" he might bring to their team, and the discrimination against him and other publicly out gay players was legitimized.

The message this sends to LGBT athletes is very clear: *If you come out publicly, or if you even come out to some teammates, you single-handedly jeopardize the season for your team. You put your career at risk.*

The alternative message the media should be sending is about leadership.

What do the examples outlined in the section above—including the Patriots and the Ravens, the Trojans and Bisons—all have in common? They are all strong programs with powerful leaders at the very top of the organization. When a college football player says, "The world would have to end to affect this team's focus," he displays an intimate understanding of leadership and team dynamics far beyond the talking heads and many of the well-paid and powerful front-office executives in professional sports.

Any coach, general manager, scout, or team president who worries him or herself with the "distraction" of a gay athlete should be fired.

I've been to the Super Bowl. It is a "distracting" mess. The media is ever-present. The host city is overrun with fans, celebrities, major corporations, and parties from dawn to dawn. The spectacle of a team simply departing its home city generates news headlines. While the teams try to quarantine their coaches and players in remote hotels, there is no escaping the hype and "distraction" that comes pouring through social media and technology.

If a team's front office cannot handle the attention a gay athlete might bring, it is woefully ill-equipped to win a world championship.

While the drumbeat about the "distraction" of a gay athlete continues, every shred of evidence, in conjunction with a gay athlete on a professional sports team, suggests a different scenario.

Few people realize the first openly gay male athlete entered

American professional sports in 2005 when the Boston Cannons of Major League Lacrosse drafted Dartmouth goalie Andrew Goldstein, who had shared his story publicly with *Outsports* and ESPN in the months leading up to the draft. Certainly the media coverage of MLL is barely even a fraction of that of the Big Five sports leagues. Still, Goldstein's groundbreaking presence in the league was such a non-distraction that the Long Island Lizards acquired him a year later.

"It isn't an issue with us," said Lizards spokesperson Scott Neiss in 2005. "We're a professional lacrosse team who drafted Andrew for his skills in the cage. His teammates are all professional about it, and he is treated like any other player by us."

When the Brooklyn Nets signed Jason Collins midway through the 2013–14 season, the "distraction" question was heavy on the minds of sports writers. The Nets responded by running off a 12–3 streak over the next month, beating the likes of the Miami Heat and the Chicago Bulls.

"This shows that 'distraction' is BS," Collins told the *New York Daily News* at the time. It was validation for the center who had for a year privately bemoaned the distraction "BS" that had, whether he wanted to admit it or not, kept NBA teams away from signing him.

When Robbie Rogers was signed by Major League Soccer's LA Galaxy, he had just come out publicly a few months earlier and quit the sport. When his signing was announced, media descended on the then–Home Depot Center for the team's announcement. Rogers proved to be such a distraction that the team went to the playoffs that season and won the MLS Cup—with Rogers starting in the final—the next year.

The conversation around Sam has focused on the distraction of his new team like no other athlete. And it was all blown desperately out of proportion.

"Absolutely not," Jeff Fisher told reporters when asked if Sam's presence at the Rams facility had been a distraction to the team. "Let's define *distraction*. There were a couple of extra cameras during early OTAs. There may have been an extra camera yesterday as rookies reported and went on the field the first time."

A couple extra cameras. Scary.

When the Dallas Cowboys signed Sam after his release from the Rams, Dallas head coach Jason Garrett reiterated the sentiment.

How much did the distraction of Sam's signing affect the Cowboys in the win-loss column? While he was on the team's practice squad, they ran off a 6–1 record. Incidentally, the Cowboys lost their first two games after releasing Sam in October 2014, and the Rams started that season 1–4 after they cut Sam.

At the time Fisher made his comments, CBS Sports, ESPN, *Sports Illustrated,* and many others wrote stories specifically about the coach's observation. The media is addicted to the story line of gay athletes being distractions, and many fans have bought into it, even if many others in sports realize what a red herring the discussion is.

As a result of the "distraction" myth, the Big Five professional sports leagues in America have taken the easy road on LGBT issues. The media, along with many LGBT activists in sports, have let them.

Each of the leagues now has some form of anti-discrimination policy that legally (but not practically) protects players and employees of different sexual orientations (though gender identity largely remains unprotected). They all have a relationship with some LGBT athlete or organization that lets them say, *Look at how inclusive we are.*

Yet none of them is executing what needs to be done to ensure gay athletes feel comfortable coming out to their teams or the public. They are doing enough to keep LGBT fans happy, with teams hosting "Pride" nights for the community and allowing logos to be painted in rainbow colors. As I said, a handful even tweeted support for same-sex marriage when the Supreme Court made marriage equality legal.

They are all doing something—none of them is doing everything.

I was at the 2014 NFL Annual Meeting in Orlando with Wade Davis. The NFL had invited Davis to speak to the owners and coaches about LGBT inclusion, and NFL spokesman Greg Aiello had asked me to attend to cover the impending drafting of Michael Sam and to ask attendees about inclusion of gay players. It was a powerful couple of days, complete with well-received conversations, smiles, and handshakes.

Two men in particular stood out to me from those meetings. The first was St. Louis Rams coach Jeff Fisher. I caught him at a snack table during a break and chatted him up about Davis's presentation. He was thrilled with it. He thought Davis had presented the information in a concise, palatable way and made the issue of sexual orientation relatable to a mostly straight, mostly over-fifty crowd. When I asked him if he would invite Davis to speak to his team later that summer he gave a big thumbs-up. Six weeks later Fisher drafted Sam and brought Davis to speak to his team. Fisher was translating the discussions at the Annual Meeting into action.

The other conversation I remember particularly clearly is one I had with then–Denver Broncos head coach John Fox. When I asked him about the presentation Davis made to the coaches, he said it opened his eyes to an issue he simply didn't know much about. He had recently watched *Dallas Buyers Club* and caught a rare glimpse (for him) into the struggles of the LGBT community. He had simply never engaged to learn, and that day he seemed over the moon that he'd gotten more education from Davis.

"I thought it was the most incredible presentation I've seen since I've been around here, and I've been here a long time," said Fox, who's been a coach in the NFL since 1989.

Fox never brought Davis to talk with the Broncos players or front office. While Davis was the NFL's handpicked presenter on the issue of LGBT inclusion, any conversations about that with the Broncos team went unguided by his expertise.

In fact, as of the 2015 football season, only three of the thirty-two teams had reached out to the NFL to invite Davis in for a conversation about inclusion of gay people since his presentation. It was easy to bring him to Orlando for a fifteen-minute talk with the owners and coaches. It was easy to ask me to join them in the hallway outside the Annual Meeting. Yet it's hard to take that message to every single one of the thirty-two NFL locker rooms.

In the two years since Davis began working with the NFL, not a single current or former player has come out publicly. Not one.

The easy road gets taken, the hard road gets bypassed.

It's the same for the NBA, NHL, and Major League Soccer. All of them have a partnership with one or two LGBT sports advocacy organizations. They all have a face to put on the issue: the NBA has Jason Collins, MLS has Robbie Rogers, and the NHL has executives Brian and Patrick Burke, who while straight have been out front on LGBT inclusion in the league. All the leagues have nondiscrimination policies.

Yet none of them has advanced the verifiable inclusion of LGBT athletes over the last two years. During Gay Pride celebrations in 2013, we had one openly gay active athlete in the Big Five who was on a team: Robbie Rogers. Two years later, we were in the exact same spot with only one active male athlete in the Big Five. They have done lovely things, but nothing they have done has brought more openly gay athletes into their leagues.

The WNBA is in a very different place, as I have discussed, with various athletes coming out publicly and the league embracing an entire LGBT Pride platform. Fifteen years ago, a WNBA executive told me there was an active push to minimize the visibility of lesbian athletes, coaches, and fans in the league, lest it scare away "straight families." That has completely transformed with the league regularly highlighting LGBT issues, partnerships, and people.

Major League Baseball comes the closest to getting it right for the men. When the league hired openly gay former Dodger and Padre Billy Bean as its Ambassador for Inclusion, executives made a powerful, public commitment to inclusion of LGBT people. The league embraced Bean, putting him up front in all of their inclusion efforts.

A stroke of genius came during 2015 spring training. While MLB had no active out players, it had Bean. Working with New York Mets general manager Sandy Alderson, Bean created an opportunity for himself to put on a Mets uniform and take the field during a practice. It put Bean on equal footing with the rest of the players for a day, in the locker room and on the field. The message of an openly gay man in a Mets uniform during spring training—both from an education and a visibility standpoint— was powerful.

The results? MLB was the only one of the Big Five men's sports leagues to have an athlete or coach—minor league pitcher David Denson with a Milwaukee Brewers farm team—come out publicly while active in the system in 2015.

Bean's participation led Mets second baseman Daniel Murphy to take exception with the "homosexual lifestyle" while embracing the opportunity to welcome Bean or any other gay teammate into his life. "I do disagree with the fact that Billy is a homosexual. That doesn't mean I can't still invest in him and get to know him. I don't think the fact that someone is a homosexual should completely shut the door on investing in them in a relational aspect."

At least Bean's presence opened a dialogue that hadn't existed on the Mets. In the following weeks Bean practiced with the Detroit Tigers, Philadelphia Phillies, and Los Angeles Dodgers. He visited a bunch more teams that season, from Tampa Bay to Oakland. When he spoke to team owners in August, he was bombarded with requests for more conversations and trainings. Bean has gone beyond the conversation about gay athletes by creating a program within Major League Baseball to recruit LGBT people into front-office roles with teams and the league office.

"We can't just focus on the athletes," Bean told me. "We can't really control who's going to come out. What we can do is recruit out students and professionals who are ready to be part of Major League Baseball."

While the NFL and NBA have engaged Davis and Collins in arm's-length partnerships, MLB has hired Bean full-time, made him a league executive, moved him to New York, and given him a full agenda. They have embraced their LGBT ambassador like no other league.

I do disagree with Bean on one point: we have more influence on who comes out and when they do it than most realize. The league commissioners, along with folks like Bean, are in powerful positions to affect change and help people out of the closet. There are important ways that they can, like Branch Rickey, help move inclusion forward. Bean has already shown this with minor league player David Denson. Bean and other power players need to work with more athletes and coaches to come out publicly if they are going to truly change the lives of LGBT people in and out of sports.

\* \* \*

Despite all of this, there is still no publicly out gay active Major League Baseball player, and there never has been. (Former Los Angeles and Oakland outfielder Glenn Burke was not publicly out while playing, despite what anyone tries to tell you.)

There is no greater measure of LGBT-inclusion efforts than the number of people who are out and proud in the workplace. Period. All of the other indicators—policy, partnerships, visibility campaigns—are means to the end. Deutsche Bank can claim to have inclusive policies, but if their LGBT employee network has a population of one, the company cannot claim to be inclusive. (Deutsche Bank, it should be noted, has many out LGBT employees.) It's the same for professional sports leagues. With approximately 4,000 athletes passing through an active roster of the Big Five in any given year, having only one publicly out athlete (0.025 percent) is a reflection of the failures of these leagues' inclusion efforts.

So with all of these initiatives, what gives?

Each one of the leagues could have a publicly out gay player by year's end if the commissioners chose to. Jackie Robinson didn't magically appear out of thin air in Major League Baseball: he was chosen by Dodgers owner Branch Rickey, who gave him all of the support and resources he needed to succeed.

Each league's commissioner—including Don Garber, who already has Rogers in Major League Soccer—should identify the gay athletes in his league and reach out to them specifically and personally. If he doesn't know who they are, he can contact me and I'll gather a small group of people to meet with him about it. He should reach out to those people and work with them toward a plan to come out publicly. He should direct the team owners and head coaches to ensure the job security of these athletes—that might sound crazy on these win-now sports teams, but it's time to stop dancing around the issue, be intentional, and be bold. He should ensure the full backing of his office and each and every one of the team owners. To advance social change you must act deliberately.

He should be to these gay athletes what Rickey was to Robinson. Anything short of this is simply lip service and buying time.

Why hasn't it happened? Why hasn't one of the commissioners, despite all of their promises and speeches about inclusion, taken proactive steps to "integrate" openly gay men into sports?

The hurdles are what I have discussed above. Older white men in suits want to pretend their sports leagues exist in a vacuum. They want to believe there is no need to address cultural issues or take on "social experiments" under their watch. If it happens? Fine, they'll deal with it. Yet none of them have displayed the spine or leadership to truly liberate his closeted gay athletes.

They are not alone. I had coffee not long ago with former WNBA president Laurel Richie. She is not a white man in a suit. She is an impressive, thoughtful African American woman in a well-appointed outfit. When she asked me what she could do to help LGBT athletes, I told her the same thing: identify as many lesbians as you can, ensure the support of team owners and the league, and help them come out publicly.

She blanched. No interest.

How ineffective are PR campaigns and lovely statements of inclusion from athletes? Consider this. No men's pro sports league in North America has done more of these than the NHL. Every team has made a You Can Play video. Many of them have held LGBT Pride nights. They have participated in pride parades. The league commissioner has embraced the LGBT community.

What's the only Big Five league that has never had an openly gay current or former player? The NHL. The PR moves simply don't translate into athletes feeling comfortable with coming out.

This dynamic goes beyond sports team executives. I've talked with Davis and various other LGBT sports activists several times about trying to convince professional athletes to come out publicly, men and women who are either retired or secure in their positions on teams. There's an incredible opportunity for them to not simply change the conversation about sports but, frankly, to make a lot of money. So far, nothing. No one.

And that's the rub. Even activists who dedicate their lives to the advocacy of equality for LGBT athletes refuse to aggressively lead coaches and athletes out of the closet. Like the front-office executives, they focus on trainings and helping to write inclusive policies that can carry their stamp. Proactively coax athletes to come out? So many people are just not comfortable with it. The power brokers in professional sports could transform the Big Five in a year if they wanted to. So far they have stayed away from this aspect of the struggle.

Without that extended hand, without people in sports taking Branch Rickey's lead and purposefully opening doors, gay male pro athletes are left with only grand pronouncements of support and occasional locker-room visits from advocates on which to build their courage. Until that changes, until these commissioners and team owners decide to truly kick down closet doors, we will likely be stuck on third base waiting for the next athlete to find his own courage to come out . . . and hopefully not be outed before he does so.

At the 2014 NFL Annual Meeting I tried to help the NFL take another important step. I know of two NFL head coaches who have gay children—one has a son, and the other has multiple gay kids. These children of NFL head coaches are out in their personal lives but have never talked publicly about the love and acceptance they may (or may not) receive from their famous dads.

At the big mid-meeting gala, attended by all of the owners,

coaches, and media, I saw one of these men standing at a table with his wife. They were in the middle of the room yet by themselves, just a dozen feet away. I made conversation with them, talking about a mutual friend of ours. When I mentioned their gay son, they froze. After a couple minutes of friendly banter about it, they loosened up; I clearly wasn't interested in grabbing a story and running with it without their permission.

"What would it take for you to talk with me about having a gay son?" I asked the coach.

"Really, it's up to him," the coach said.

"Cool. Well, can you connect me with him? I'd love to reach out and see if he'd be willing to share."

He took my card. I never heard from him.

The next day I saw the other coach in the hallway. He was with the team's head of public relations. I chatted him up and eased into the topic of his gay kids.

"That's really private business," he said to me, shooting daggers with his eyes.

"I totally understand," I replied. "But I'm sure you know the incredible impact you all could have if you all talked about it."

He kept glaring at me, then said calmly, "It's up to them."

It was déjà vu. "Awesome. Can you connect me with them?"

"No, I'm sorry. I can't."

Two powerful men in sports. Both with gay kids. Both unwilling to help advance the conversation about inclusion. There's another Super Bowl–winning head coach who has a gay brother. He's never spoken publicly about it. Roger Goodell was the NFL commissioner for six years before he decided to talk about his gay brother. With so much reticence from men whose family members are directly impacted, it should be no wonder that other team owners, general managers, and head coaches frankly couldn't give a shit.

More than two years after my conversations with these men, neither of the coaches has proactively spoken publicly in support of gay athletes, same-sex marriage, or anything of the sort. What's worse, one of them dismissed the notion that Sam's sexual orientation might be why he wasn't with an NFL team shortly after being cut by the Rams, ignoring the continuing undercurrents of homophobia in men's professional sports.

Far more important for them has been the NFL's underlying mantra: *Don't. Rock. The. Boat.*

# The Rumors and Outing That Follow Guys Like Troy Aikman, Aaron Rodgers, and Tim Tebow

*I have no idea if Tim Tebow is gay*. I have no idea if Troy Aikman is gay. I have no idea if Aaron Rodgers is gay.

With all of that said, many sports fans seem to wonder about all three of them. I've written columns on all of these guys, each one asking, "Is [insert athlete's name] gay?" Every time one of these men is on television, the readership on that story skyrockets. During the college football national championship game between Ohio State and Oregon, our most-read story of the day—thanks to his on-air appearances—was a piece questioning Tebow's sexual orientation. That story beat out several others on the inclusive messages of the Ohio State athletic department and Oregon football coach Mark Helfrich. All of that was of distant interest to the sexual orientation of a college football commentator from Florida flashing across the screen.

To be sure, I've gotten criticism for writing these columns. "You shouldn't be outing people," some of the attacks charge. I'm not, and I never have. I have no evidence of the sexual orientation of any of these men. I've heard speculation about guys like Brady Anderson and Terrell Owens and Steve Young. I've been told *rock-solid, surefire, swear-to-God* stories about each one of them. Yet Young's been married for years, Anderson once dated a female friend of mine, and Owens pursued my sister. (None of this says they don't like men, but chances are slim any of them are certifiably gay.) For the most part I brush off the speculation and imagined stories, usually coming from gay men who are more purveyors of wishful thinking than insiders with intimate knowledge.

Yet the conversations are out there. People wonder about these athletes—and it's not just gay people wondering. Whether it's from Dallas fans or national radio hosts, there is not a single question I've gotten more over the last fifteen years than, *Is Troy Aikman gay?*

Aikman's journey down this road all started years ago when a sportsclown named Skip Bayless penned a book called *Hell-Bent: The Crazy Truth About the "Win or Else" Dallas Cowboys.* In the book Bayless shared his conversations with a couple of Cowboys who allegedly believed that their Hall of Fame quarterback, Aikman, was gay. Mind you, Bayless never said Aikman was gay; rather, he shared that some people on the team were suspicious.

"All I heard from people around the country who didn't read the book was, *You outed Troy Aikman?*" Bayless told website *The Starting Five* in 2009. "I didn't. The coach [Barry Switzer] definitely thought he was gay and a lot of his teammates thought he was gay."

Aikman has not hidden his hatred for the speculation over the years. He's said he's not sure what he would do if he saw Bayless again—many people taking that as a not-so-veiled physical threat. Aikman has called being gay a "lifestyle" that people choose. His less-than-welcoming response to the news every time has earned him a bit more snarky speculation.

While Aikman has voiced his displeasure with the stories, there's nothing wrong with the speculation about an athlete's sexual orientation, because—news flash—there's nothing wrong with being gay. It's not accusing someone of breaking a law, it's not accusing someone of hurting anyone. There's no libel, no defamation. The wondering aloud if someone loves men or women or both is, largely, harmless fun. Sure, there are some religious folks who continue to harbor resentment against gay people in this country, but they are now in a distinct minority. In America today, with a multitude of people who are out and proud, and the power of the media and other for-profit companies that share their stories and support them, there is nothing wrong with being gay.

Years ago, *Outsports* was sued because an allegedly straight amateur athlete claimed that by posting his photograph on our site we were calling him gay. He sued us in North Carolina, where the law specifically states that calling someone gay is neither libel nor defamation. Even North Carolina a decade ago knew that calling someone gay wasn't a bad thing.

In the case of the subjects of my "Is So-and-So Gay" columns, I'm not even calling them gay, I'm simply wondering aloud if they are. Heck, I'm barely wondering aloud—I'm reflecting a question circulating around social media and giving some insight as to why fans are engaged in the debate.

I'm also not simply pulling the names of athletes out of thin air and speculating about their sexual orientation. I've never heard anyone suggest—publicly or privately—that LeBron James is gay. Or Pau Gasol. Or Ben Roethlisberger. Or thousands of other athletes. I don't write, *Is Pedro Martínez gay?* because I've never heard a single person wonder about it—to write that piece would be starting a conversation that simply doesn't exist in the public realm. I have no interest in that, and there's no public interest in it either.

Yet with these three men in particular—Tebow, Rodgers, and Aikman—the speculation about their sexual orientation is private and public, on Google and Twitter, across media and ages and races like no other.

And there's nothing wrong with that.

* * *

It's interesting to look at the differences between the reactions athletes and actors have when people wonder if they are gay.

Patrick Stewart, the actor of *Star Trek* and *X-Men* fame, told the *Advocate*—the nation's largest LGBT news publication—that he was "utterly flattered" by the "distinctive honor" of being assumed to be gay.

Joel McHale, best known for his role on the TV show *Community*, shared the same sentiment, wondering why someone wouldn't feel that way. "If a guy gets offended by that, there's something wrong with him," McHale told the *Advocate*. "I take it as a compliment."

The only person upset by speculation about singer and actor Nick Jonas, who said he was eager to do a gay sex scene if a script called for it, was Adam Lambert. The gay singer seemed to feel threatened by Jonas's encroachment on his gay audience. *Anyone find it interesting how straight male Pop stars r pandering to gay audiences lately!? Should we be flattered?* Lambert asked on social media.

Jonas couldn't care less about gay men ogling him or thinking wishfully that he were gay.

Then there are these three athletes.

"I'm upset about it because it was made up and there was nothing accurate about anything that was insinuated," Aikman told *Sports Illustrated* in early 2015. "It is ridiculous, and, yeah, it bothers me. If that is a lifestyle people choose, so be it."

Aaron Rodgers simply refused to entertain the notion: "I'm just gonna say, I'm not gay. I really, really like women. That's all I can say about that."

Actually, he could have said so much more about gay people being okay and him being flattered by the suggestion, but he chose not to. He did finally offer something supportive in early

2016, saying he doesn't agree with homophobic language.

Tebow has simply refused to answer any questions about being gay. When one reporter I know secured an interview with him, the only off-limit topic was sexual orientation.

These guys have tried to keep the chatter as far away from them as possible. Their responses could have been powerful, uplifting. Such as: "I know there are a lot of gay people out there who have experienced so much hate and rejection, and my heart really goes out to them. Frankly, if someone wants to think I'm gay, I'm cool with it as long as they support me and the Green Bay Packers."

Instead they get offended and clam up.

For the record, I won't get upset if anyone calls me straight. Hell, my husband would get a kick out of it.

Even so, it's still important to give athletes the benefit of the doubt before writing speculation stories about their sexual orientation. Just like outing someone who isn't ready to be "out" could have negative repercussions for the athlete and the public, reckless speculation by people like Jim Buzinski or me would be just kind of . . . shitty.

When speculation bubbled up about Rodgers in late 2013, shortly after he and his roommate, well, "broke up," I held back my pen. I had heard rumors about Rodgers dating men back to his days at Cal, but even as others wrote about what certainly looked like a jilted lover cat-scratching Rodgers on social media, Jim and I waited. Once Rodgers made a public comment about it on a radio show, it became fair game.

Same thing with Kerry Rhodes. The then–Arizona Cardinals safety got put on blast by a man who claimed to be his lover. He released photos of the two getting quite cozy while they were allegedly dating, and the gossip sites ran with it. We didn't touch it for a while, which drew some criticism from readers claiming all kinds of homophobia on our part for not talking about Rhodes. When he made a public statement on the matter, we addressed it. In early 2016, actress Nicky Whelan announced she was set to marry Rhodes, prompting the *Daily Mail*'s headline, "That's a Surprise!"

We've taken the same tactic with former Mets catcher Mike Piazza, former Falcons fullback Ovie Mughelli, and several others.

The biggest reason we held back on these before publishing any kind of story about them possibly being gay was our gut sense about the likelihood of the speculation being true. While I don't find anything wrong with light-hearted speculation, it does carry a different gravitas when the person being discussed is actually gay. If I think there's a reasonable chance, I wait. Not looking like a click-bait gossip doesn't hurt, either.

It's not outing, but it's reckless speculation if you think there's a good chance that rumors about a gay athlete are true. I know how hard it is to be patient about posting stories in this age of rewards for the fastest tweeter, but sometimes waiting for the subject to make a comment first is the best policy.

With that said, I have rarely been more tempted than when New York Giants wide receiver Odell Beckham Jr. claimed late in the 2015 NFL season that players on a number of teams had targeted him with gay slurs. There was certainly speculation about why his opponents would target him this way. It was easy to dismiss it as being due to his blond highlights and penchant for dancing. Beckham just isn't one of these desperately macho guys who, like so many in the NFL, are constantly looking to "prove his manhood." That could certainly be what other players are picking up on.

Still, it was the aftermath that got many people wondering what this was really all about. If these accusations were true, why didn't Beckham speak publicly about them? (One thing he did do was talk to guys like Michael Irvin and Deion Sanders, who did the dirty work for him.) Why didn't he raise the issue in his NFL hearing on his suspension for illegally hitting Carolina Panthers cornerback Josh Norman? And why didn't the Giants organization, with its long history of supporting LGBT issues, pursue the allegations?

It was a head-scratcher that drove me to start writing an "Is Odell Beckham Jr. gay?" column. With Jim's urging, I thought better of it and shifted gears. Still, the questions surrounding that strange incident linger in the minds of many.

*Outsports* has had one very clear policy from the first day we published the website: we will not publicly out anyone. Period.

Coming out is a personal decision because, while it has very powerful public effects, it also has very personal implications. For the general public, Jason Collins and Brittney Griner are people on television who play sports several months a year. It's often easy to forget that these athletes have family members and friends— personal relationships that are affected by their identities. I've talked with countless young athletes who want to come out publicly, but when they don't have their personal lives in order it's a big red flag.

"Do your parents know?" I always ask. Sometimes it's a yes, sometimes it's a no, and often it's, "Well, Mom knows but we haven't told Dad yet." I always make sure both parents know before we move forward: the people in an athlete's personal life have to hear it from them first. It was true of Michael Sam, who told his father just days before he came out publicly, and it's true for every other athlete moving forward.

While most of the public believes everyone in professional sports lives in Beverly Hills and drives a Maserati, most athletes

who come out are in high school or college, and most professional athletes still struggle to keep up with the bills, particularly
after their careers are over. They aren't born with silver spoons in
their mouths—they have grounded, real-world budget problems.
If someone believes that making their sexual orientation public
knowledge will cost them some of that usually hard-earned and
often much-needed cash, it's no one else's right to change their
dynamic for them.

At times I have advised LGBT athletes to avoid any kind of
public declaration of their sexual orientation. While Middle Tennessee State placekicker Alan Gendreau was out to much of his
team by the time he hit his senior season, he and I talked at length
about coming out publicly. At the time he had hopes of a shot
at the NFL, and that was within his reach: he was on pace to set
school and Sun Belt Conference records, and he did. When you're
a potential NFL prospect at a marginal position, the last thing
you want to do is give a team any reason to reconsider offering
you a shot at your dream. Gendreau wasn't the SEC Defensive
Player of the Year, he was a kicker from the Sun Belt. It was tough
to recommend he come out publicly before his senior season. A
poor season for the Blue Raiders, a couple blocked kicks, and
limited opportunities scuttled his best chance at the NFL, and he
came out publicly a year after graduating.

While there is that exception like Gendreau, I spend most
of my time trying to convince athletes to come out. Given that
coming out is their choice, my only option is to convince them to
do it. We're at the point where LGBT athletes coming out is the
only way to advance the conversation in meaningful ways and en
masse. If you're not showing athletes and coaches open doors to
coming out, you're sitting on the sidelines.

Convince someone to come out on their own terms. Don't
out them.

To be clear, "outing" an athlete is something very specific that has to meet three criteria.

First, there has to be a public statement that someone is LGBT. I say "public" because it's nearly impossible to not privately out someone en route to a story they've asked to be written. When Michael Sam was planning his public coming-out, Howard Bragman told me about him. (Howard wanted my help in planning the strategy of the story.) I told my husband about Michael, and I also told Jim Buzinski, my business partner. Was that "outing" Sam to my personal and professional partners? Yeah. Was that really a crime? Hardly. These were two confidantes who frankly had to know what was coming, just as Bragman had to bring me into the loop. With a "no-outing" rule, to break the rule, the "outing" has to be public or with the intention of making it public.

Second, it has to be without the person's explicit permission. I've written about hundreds of LGBT athletes, coaches, administrators, executives, and members of the sports media who want to come out. When their own will is behind the sharing of their sexual orientation, there's no wrongdoing: it's not "outing," it's them "coming out."

Behind my private sharing of Sam's big news before his big day was the athlete's desire to ultimately make it public. There are various professional athletes I know to be gay. I have not shared their names with my husband or anyone else, though I've been asked a hundred times. I don't have their permission and they don't want to be outed to anyone. It wouldn't be right to share their story with anyone, especially in a public manner.

Finally, there has to be knowledge that the information is true. If you don't know someone's gay, then you can't "out" them. If someone's straight and you say they're gay, you haven't outed them, you've just been trolling or having fun or speculating or any one of a bunch of descriptions for it. If you've heard rumors and innuendos, as is the case for me with more professional athletes than I could possibly name, you're just talking about "speculation."

I've wondered about Troy Aikman's sexual orientation publicly on various occasions. I have no idea if the man is gay. Without proof and certitude, there is no outing.

Some people argue there are rare occasions when an outing is justified. While it's still definitively an "outing," it comes without earned moral outrage. According to this line of thinking, the right to stay in the closet is forfeited when an LGBT person does something publicly anti-gay. If someone is fighting against equality for LGBT people, the thought process goes, they have earned the ire of the LGBT community and forfeited the right to hypocrisy.

Barney Frank, the gay former congressman from Massachusetts, was part of a scandal in the late eighties when his lover (or boyfriend or roommate or whatever he was) ran a prostitution ring out of Frank's home. Since then Frank has been a leading voice in the government for LGBT equality. On the other side of the issue—usually on the other side of the aisle from the stalwart Democrat—Frank has faced opposition by closeted gay people who fight against gay rights to appease their supporters.

In those cases, when a closeted gay person is actually fighting against his or her own rights and doing so simply for personal political gain, Frank argues it's completely moral and just to out that person publicly. It has come to be known as "The Frank Rule."

"I think there's a right to privacy," Frank told TV host Bill Maher in 2006. "But the right to privacy should not be a right to hypocrisy. And people who want to demonize other people shouldn't then be able to go home and close the door and do it themselves."

When Alabama lawmakers fought against a February 2015 court order to recognize same-sex marriage in the state, out lesbian state representative Patricia Todd threatened to expose the extramarital affairs of the very people who wanted to keep gay marriage illegal. *I will not stand by and allow legislators to talk about "family values" when they have affairs, and I know of many who are and have,* Todd wrote on Facebook.

Even more than the bigotry itself, it seems hypocrisy changes the game for a lot of gay people.

The "pioneer" of public outings is writer and radio host Michelangelo Signorile, who turned the tactic into an artform in the late eighties and early nineties. Signorile has earned a reputation taking on homophobia of any kind at any turn from anyone. Guns N' Roses attracted Signorile's attention when in 1988 they released the song "One in a Million," with the lyrics, *"Immigrants and faggots/They make no sense to me/They come to our country/And . . . spread some fuckin' disease."* The band's label boss was none other than David Geffen, who at the time was closeted. Signorile took aim at Geffen, outing him to the world as a gay man. (Geffen has since acknowledged that he's gay.) Signorile outed other powerful LGBT people he believed to be damaging hypocrites on gay issues, including gossip columnist Liz Smith and *Forbes* magazine publisher Malcolm Forbes.

Which brings us to sports.

Athletes play games. That is their public role. Yes, they act as role models and, yes, they have powerful spheres of influence. But ultimately they are not writing laws like anti-gay politicians. They aren't creating messages in TV shows or films or music like anti-gay artists. They throw footballs. They swing bats. Anti-gay people in sports can have a lot of power if they choose to, but most of them opt to keep politics at arm's length.

When they enter into the political arena, à la Tony Dungy raising money to fight against same-sex marriage rights in Indiana, they may open themselves up to "The Frank Rule." But as long as they're just playing their sport and not venturing into political activism, even if they were to make anti-gay comments, I don't think "The Frank Rule" can generally apply to athletes, coaches, and the like.

Still, I've certainly thought about invoking "The Frank Rule" once or twice.

My most recent consideration involves ESPN personality Israel Gutierrez whom I knew to be gay. He was even engaged to marry his boyfriend, yet on radio and television he "played" a straight guy, as though he was an actor hired for a role on the Especially for Straights Programming Network. During one particular appearance in 2014, he played a straight guy grossed out by having his feet massaged by another man. Straight guys are supposed to want massages from women, not men; I've yet to find a gay man who doesn't prefer a masseur to a masseuse. Sure, athletes are massaged by men all the time, but when it's not in the training room they're supposed to be sickened by the idea. Gutierrez played the "straight dude" role that day, even while he was hitting the gay bars in South Florida with his fiancé.

When I tweeted a question about what to do with him—without using his name, of course—many people said homophobic actions by someone in sports gave me the license to out him. I didn't. I wouldn't. Instead, Gutierrez shared the following blog post the week before his wedding in September 2015, finally coming out to the world:

> *I've been agonizing for months trying to figure out how to do this. It's been incredibly difficult, to the point where I usually talk myself in circles and end up making very little sense. So I decided on this simple blog entry. No formalities, no restrictions, just me letting you into a portion of my life I've kept largely separate from my professional career. I'm gay, which*

*plenty of people, I'm sure, have either deduced or just guessed as much over the years. But this isn't me "coming out." The truth is, I've been out to friends and family for more than six years.*

After agonizing for months and finally posting the story, the reaction was supportive and overwhelming. If I had outed him, chances are the reaction would have been quite different. Gutierrez was able to come out in his own time, and this made all the difference in the world.

While I don't and won't out athletes, I want to.

When Robbie Rogers came out publicly, then made his way back to Major League Soccer as an openly gay man, a young soccer player in West Virginia named Michael Martin took notice. Martin was a high school soccer goalie struggling with his sexual orientation. In Rogers he saw himself—a young athlete trying to find his way in their sport. Watching Rogers march out of the closet inspired Martin to do the same. In high school. In West Virginia. By dancing with the homecoming king.

Helping kids like Martin is why I do what I do, waking up every day to connect with young LGBT people in sports and to drive stories that will inspire them. Each of those stories helps someone else, who helps someone else . . . It's a powerful domino effect.

Yet for every Michael Martin coming out in a West Virginia high school, there are dozens of professional athletes who have chosen to not help inspire more kids like him. I understand the circumstances that keep some of these closeted athletes quiet. They're journeymen. They're concerned about their future after they turn twenty-six. I've said for years I would never tell a pro athlete in the first year of his career that he should come out publicly because of the possibility of it affecting his career. Michael Sam coming out when he did—his entire career ahead of him and no assurance of any payday—was an incredibly courageous anomaly.

Then there are a bunch of millionaire athletes in their thirties, with a decade of playing in their league and more assets and money than they could spend in two lifetimes, who choose to stay closeted so they can make more money and build their "legacy." The choice they make is simple: inspiring LGBT youth, who experience the highest suicide rate of any demographic under twenty, is less important than playing one more season in Major League Baseball or getting that next endorsement deal. They tell themselves and the people around them that they want to be remembered as "a great hitter," not "a great *gay* hitter."

They are desperately stuck in their own homophobia.

What's worse are the retired athletes who refuse to come out. I know a Hall of Fame athlete with a longtime partner who simply refuses to come out. Addicted to his "legacy," he fears the attention may go away, the phone calls may stop. He thinks his career will suddenly become a side note to his sexual orientation. Given his impeccable resume, it's nonsense, but that's the irrational fear he lives with.

This all makes me crazy. So many people dedicate their lives to helping these youth, millions of whom feel marginalized and alone. As I've said, these kids are many times more likely to attempt suicide. Often they are driven from sports because they're told they don't belong. Yet these privileged millionaire athletes can't find it in themselves to provide a role model, to give the kids reassurances about themselves. A select few—Jason Collins, Brittney Griner, Robbie Rogers, Seimone Augustus—have taken the leap. Every single one who adds his name to the list changes the game for thousands of youth. There need to be many, many more.

Ultimately, what holds me back from outing these athletes is 1) what I believe to be a certain right to privacy, and 2) the possibility of outing the "wrong" person. What if someone isn't ready to handle the reaction in their personal and professional lives? What if the person who means the most to them—their mother, their grandfather, an old college buddy—reacts badly to it? What if they don't have the personal fortitude to handle some ribbing that bubbles over in the locker room? What if their reaction to being outed actually does damage to LGBT youth? Only the athlete herself knows if she can handle it—that's why it's up to her when she shares that very personal secret with the world.

The actions of and reactions to Israel Gutierrez are a perfect example of the power of *not* outing someone before he or she is ready.

# 10 Ahman Green Unlocks the Media's Fear of "The Question"

*I had been trying for years* to get sports writers at the biggies—*ESPN, New York Times*—and beat writers at other publications to ask athletes about gay issues. They just weren't interested. Sure, when an athlete like John Amaechi came out publicly, a few of them would use the news hook to ask a cursory "How do you feel about it?" question. Sports reporters generally gave me three main reasons they just wouldn't ask athletes questions about gay issues.

First, they assumed that it wouldn't end well. Athletes were homophobic jerks, or at least that's what these reporters remember from their high school and college days in the seventies, eighties, and nineties. The last thing an athlete wanted to do was answer questions about "fags."

Second, because of that belief they didn't want to alienate a source. One of the things that separates sports reporters from fans is access. Sports reporters are, for the most part, fans with an audience. Many of them today are not trained journalists, though there are some great sports journalists today like the *New York Times'* John Branch and the *Nation's* Dave Zirin. But a lot of sports reporters aren't looking to uncover truths, they're interested in talking with their sports heroes and sharing their love of sports with the world. They don't want to investigate the big leagues, they want to cozy up to them. Alienating one of said heroes with questions about fags in which they have no interest? Not a chance.

Lastly, they just didn't think questions about gays had anything to do with sports. In the sports vacuum, athletes catch touchdowns, block shots, and swing bats. If it didn't have to do with a game, it wasn't right to ask. Sure, the occasional athlete would get caught killing someone or beating his wife—if there was a real hook relating directly to the athlete, reporters' questions might venture away from the Xs and Os. Randomly asking athletes "non-sports" questions about gays because you and your readers are intrigued? No, man, not gonna happen.

That reticence on the part of the media perpetuated the very notion that all athletes were homophobic and all sports were unwelcoming to LGBT athletes. All of us who played high school basketball or kicked around a soccer ball in gym class heard the language the jocks used. We saw how gay people were portrayed as the antithesis of those jocks by people in entertainment. If high school sports stars were the furthest thing from show-tune-loving queers, NBA players were a million miles further. Because reporters wouldn't ask questions about the thoughts of current athletes on these issues, we were left with our impressions from high school in the eighties and nineties.

It became clear that if anyone was going to ask well-known professional athletes how they felt about gay teammates and same-sex marriage, I would have to do it myself. And if I wasn't going to do it myself, I needed to shut up and stop asking anyone else.

The first opportunity to dive in headfirst was the 2012 NFLPA Rookie Premiere event—a few days in Los Angeles right after the NFL draft designed to showcase and educate the rookies. As I said in the introduction, the NFLPA hosted a veterans flag football game at UCLA that year featuring guys like Eddie George, Jevon Kearse, and Jesse Palmer.

As I watched these guys toss around the pigskin a few yards

from me, I finally understood the fear that held back so many other journalists from asking a couple of simple questions about the gays. With the clock ticking down to zero in the flag football game, my stomach tied itself in knots. Was I really going to ask them these questions? Was I really going to walk out into the middle of a field, grab a guy I'd only seen on TV, and ask him how he feels about two men kissing?

I convinced myself that it wasn't the "right time" to ask questions like this. "These guys aren't prepared" for these questions. My fear overwhelmed me, and I started toward the exit.

Something stopped me. I realized that if I walked off that field without having talked to any of the players about these issues, I had failed as a journalist, I had failed as an advocate, I had failed as a gay man, and I had failed the kids across the country who were unknowingly counting on me to generate conversation.

So I turned back around. Ahman Green, the former Green Bay Packers running back, was about ten feet away, kneeling by himself as he changed out of his cleats. He had just made some former NFL players look silly as he juked his way toward the end zone in the game. He seemed like he hadn't lost a step since he led the NFL in rushing almost ten years earlier. It was my moment of truth. I blurted out the words so fast, I'm surprised Green could understand them.

"Hey, Ahman, I'm from *Outsports*. We cover mostly gay issues in sports, and homophobia in sports. Have you ever had a gay teammate?"

There. Phew. I threw it out there. Now I just had to watch for his hands swinging at my head. Surely he'd try to slug me, just as other reporters had feared. Maybe I was hinting that he was gay. Maybe I was coming on to him. Whatever was going through his head, I was ready to duck.

"In our sport, to be honest, I think it would be hard for any guy to come out while he's playing," Green replied. "And that's not a happy thing to say. The gay community is just like every-body else, but they're treated differently. It's a double standard. If a guy was gay, he wouldn't come out while he was playing. He knows the possibility of the scrutiny he might face from the locker room, which would be unfair. I am very open-minded. It is what it is. People are born that way. You can't control it. Just like you're white, I'm black. But a lot of people don't think my way. I wish they did, because then there wouldn't be guys who wanted to stay hidden."

Huh? I'm sorry, what did you just say? I thought NFL players were deeply homophobic, ready to drive a gay teammate from the locker room the first time he glances at a dropped towel.

"Social change has been coming around for the last twenty to thirty years," Green continued. "I was born in 1977. A lot has changed since 1977 from issues with sports, with government, with social issues like this. I'm a big advocate of people, let them live. They're just like us. They want to live. They want to have a family. And to give somebody a headache just because that's the way they live, that's unfair just like it was back in the sixties with white and black issues. Same type of stuff."

Ummmm . . . excuse me? You're Ahman Green. You carried the football for Brett Favre. A lot. On the NFL all-time rushing yards list you're in the Top 40, ahead of Roger Craig and Larry Csonka. You're the Green Bay Packers' franchise leader in career rushing yards, yards in a season, and rushing yards in a game. You. Are. The. Man. And from one of the most-storied franchises in the NFL. You're not just answering my questions, you're waxing poetic on them.

Not knowing where to go next, I asked him if he had any gay friends or family members.

"My half-sister, my wife has several cousins. And I had a girlfriend in high school, her mom's friend was a gay guy. And it was no problem."

Did you just say your sister is a lesbian?

"Yeah. We didn't find out until she got older. She didn't come out to us. I just found out two to three years ago. We were talking through Facebook. I was looking at her pictures on Facebook, and I was seeing rainbows, and I was like, okay, I know what that means. There was another girl in her pictures. And I was like, all right, cool."

Green also told me his brother was gay. Despite having a child with his former girlfriend, his brother eventually came out, also in the last couple of years.

"That's what society forces gay people to do—to hide. Eventually they're like, forget it, man, this is how I want to live, and let it be known. So I can breathe."

As we talked, the interview reminded me of the first time Michael Irvin told me about his brother. It was slightly guarded, in passing. But he quickly warmed up and was so thrilled to have someone to talk to about it. For guys like Irvin and Green, it just took someone to ask the question for them to let out years of pent-up frustration along with thoughtful comments on the issue.

The only qualm Green had with his gay siblings was the fact that they waited so long to tell him they were gay.

He thanked me for the chat and headed on his way. I stood there for a few moments, my head spinning, trying to grasp what had just happened. I spoke to a couple other guys on the field that afternoon—Kearse told me about his gay cousin and Palmer about his gay friends. But the conversation with Green lingered in my head.

That night I worked the red carpet of an NFLPA party. Everybody was there. The first guy to come down the red carpet? Ahman Green. I realized after Green had walked away that afternoon that I had forgotten he played college ball at Nebraska, where Ron Brown coached. Brown was a powerful public opponent of equality for gay people, testifying against LGBT equal-rights laws in Nebraska. When Green came through the red carpet he saw me and said hello. I asked him about Brown.

"I just knew he was a good coach," he said. "He motivated us to be the best we could be on that football field, and anything outside of that, he always tried to teach us to be a well-rounded person."

I asked Green if he'd heard about Brown's anti-gay comments. That's when I was smacked in the head with reality.

"Hey, I didn't know you were going to ask these questions," someone hired by the NFLPA to manage the red carpet cut in. "You can't ask those questions here."

"What's wrong with these questions?" I responded. The other reporters around me were all watching me now. Someone had even put a camera on me. This was about to get good.

"Those questions aren't appropriate here. You're making people uncomfortable—"

Green put up his hand. "Excuse me," he said to the NFLPA rep, "but the only person uncomfortable is you. Now I'm having a conversation with my man Cyd here. So leave us alone and let us finish."

And with that, Green transformed how I, *Outsports,* and eventually the larger-scale sports media would handle gay issues going forward. That night, and a couple months later at the ESPY award ceremony, I would interview the biggest names in sports and ask them every question about gay athletes and marriage. Kurt Warner. Robert Griffin III. Trent Richardson. Mike Modano. Cedric Ceballos. Takeo Spikes. Even Rob Gronkowski.

We would push this issue now publicly, knowing it simply

wasn't the taboo subject the mainstream sports media had made it out to be. Athletes were willing—and sometimes excited—to talk about it.

As I've interviewed more and more athletes over the years, it's become crystal clear that the idea of the desperately homophobic professional athlete has been one of the most overblown myths in our society. To a large extent, it was members of the media themselves who created the notion. Not only were they not asking the questions of athletes, trying to get to the truth of the matter, but they have collectively built a dynamic in which the athletes don't trust them, particularly on issues like this.

Athletes have watched the media take comments from individuals and burn them all at the stake. John Rocker became tied inextricably to homophobia and racism after comments he made to a *Sports Illustrated* writer in 1999. Tim Hardaway became the face of homophobia in 2007 when he proclaimed, "I hate gay people." I've heard others suggest that Chris Culliver single-handedly torpedoed the San Francisco 49ers' chances of winning Super Bowl XLVII when he told a radio show days before the Super Bowl that he didn't want a gay teammate.

When I asked Houston Texans wide receiver DeAndre Hopkins about the stereotype of the homophobic athlete, he turned it around on me. "Like your job," he said, "a lot of people might be like, *Oh, he's an interviewer, he's a douchebag.* It's just a stereotype we get. It's sad, but oh well."

Gronkowski drove that message home for me. The bigger-than-life goofball was already tearing up the NFL for the Patriots, and had just set the single-season record for touchdowns by a tight end, when he sauntered past me on the red carpet at the ESPYs. I had already talked to a dozen athletes that day, all of them willing to answer my questions.

So when "Gronk" said he didn't want to talk to me, I was puzzled. As we got into it, he said he was just afraid of saying something wrong. You can understand why. In his rookie season he appeared in a photograph with a porn actress; he was forced to apologize. Hours after losing Super Bowl XLVI, he was seen dancing shirtless at the Patriots' postgame party; many fans and some in the media took him to task for what they foolishly deemed "celebrating a loss."

Plus, nobody gets on your case about saying the wrong thing like the gays. People who utter "sexual preference" are quickly reprimanded. Referencing "homosexuals" instead of "gay people" has become taboo. To Gronkowski, a guy with little filter who has no problem speaking his mind, the interview spelled certain doom.

Yet after reconsidering, Gronk walked back to me on the red carpet. He didn't have to. San Diego Charger Takeo Spikes and the folks at Young Hollywood, a multimedia entertainment company, were right next to me, wrangling him for an interview as well (as was pretty much everyone on the red carpet that day). After thinking about it for a moment, he gave me time for two questions.

"Have you ever played with a gay teammate?" I asked.

He mulled this over and then said he didn't know of any.

"How would you feel if one of your teammates on the Patriots came out of the closet this season?"

This time he didn't pause.

"If that's how they are, that's how they are," Gronkowski said. "I mean, we're teammates, so as long as he's being a good teammate and being respectful and everything, that's cool."

Gronk knows the love-hate relationship pro athletes have with the media does have that *love* part. While there's certainly mistrust there, the media has also turned guys like Gronkowski into multimillion-dollar marketing machines. As long as you're not saying, "I hate gay people," or some iteration of that, the publicity can be very good.

For gay athletes, the media presents identical dynamics that play out in strikingly different ways.

There aren't any LGBT athletes I know of in the last two decades who have been outed in the media against their will. There have been countless athletes, from high school soccer players to professional basketball players, who have willingly come out in the media. And there have been some athletes who have been outed by teammates or lawsuits. Yet not since Martina Navratilova in 1981 has a professional athlete I know of been outed by someone in the media. Even in Navratilova's case, she had come out in an interview to the *New York Daily News*; they simply ran the article before she wanted them to.

Even so, there's a fear within closeted athletes that someone in the media is going to out them. Despite a policy at *Outsports* that we will not out any athletes, and despite years of building trust with LGBT athletes behind the scenes, there are many in the closet who still won't talk to me for fear I'll share their secret. The trust level is so low for these men and women that their fear of the media dictates their actions.

When Michael Sam was tearing up the SEC en route to the conference's Defensive Player of the Year Award in 2013, he did not do a single media interview. He avoided press conferences the entire season. It got to the point where the media in Missouri were becoming frustrated with Sam, many of them "in the know" on his sexual orientation with no interest in reporting it without his consent.

What they could have easily done, and what I had previously advocated journalists doing, was ask Sam if he was gay. Coming from the perspective of a reporter, it made a lot of sense to ask athletes if they were gay. While it wasn't a strictly "sports question," gay athletes were increasingly becoming news. The public wanted to know more gay athletes. So asking athletes if they're gay?

The "Why not?" was what kept Sam away from the media his senior season with Missouri: he didn't want to answer that question. He wanted to keep his private life private, between him and his teammates. Fans and reporters didn't need to know whom he was dating. The fear of being asked "the question" kept him far away from the microphones and cameras after every game his senior season.

That all changed when Sam believed someone in the media was about to out him. After the season, around the time of the 2014 Senior Bowl, reporters and NFL scouts began asking him questions that made it evident they knew he was gay and they wanted him to talk about it. One sports publication allegedly sent a writer to the Senior Bowl just to try to get the story. Certainly Sam could have held onto the hope that journalists would continue to abide by the same code they hadn't broken since Navratilova.

Yet with so many bloggers with little traditional media training, and the increasing power of the "page view," on top of the guaranteed attention for any writer to break the story of an NFL prospect being gay, Sam chose to get ahead of the media, select a couple writers and outlets he and his team could trust, and tell his story *his* way.

I always thought Peter King was a homophobic jerk. I felt there was a dismissive way with which he handled gay issues in the NFL, kind of matter-of-fact with seemingly little compassion. I always thought that dismissive mentality was simply more code for homophobia.

When *Sports Illustrated*'s initial coverage of Michael Sam's coming-out largely revolved around how it was going to hurt him, that increased my distrust of King. Void in the *SI* reporting of anonymous NFL front-office sources was any notion that what those NFL team execs were saying—that Sam would drop down their boards—was wrong either practically or morally.

King sharpened his knives for Sam when the docuseries by Oprah Winfrey featuring Sam was announced. King was a shark with blood in the water.

"I just think he is sending mixed messages," King said of Sam. "He said at the scouting combine, and I quote, *I wish you guys*, meaning reporters, *would see me as a football player and not a gay football player*. Well, how many football players or gay football players are followed around by documentarians when they get drafted in the seventh round? So clearly he's not just a football player, he's something bigger. Which is fine, but don't tell us to *just treat me like a football player*."

King wanted to have his proverbial cake and eat it too.

Of King's entire response, the most telling three words were: "don't tell us." Yes, Michael Sam had said he just wanted to be known as a player. But the media didn't listen. When it was convenient for King and ESPN and NFL Network and everyone else, they made Sam a lot more than just a football player: they tried to make him "the gay Jackie Robinson."

To play off of the man's own words, how many seventh-round draft picks have ever led King's very own postdraft column? None. The title of King's column on Monday, May 12, 2014, hours after Sam was drafted: "The 2014 NFL Draft: Sealed with a Kiss."

King listed Sam's roller-coaster weekend—culminating in the kiss heard 'round the world—as the top story of the draft.

Sam didn't do that. King did.

Yet forty-eight hours later he lashed out at Sam for daring to be anything but a football player "drafted in the seventh round."

ESPN's Kate Fagan took aim at Sam after he walked away from the Montreal Alouettes. Citing *Dancing with the Stars* and media appearances, Fagan said, "The truth is that Sam distracted himself. Actually, that's not precise enough: Sam allowed himself to be distracted."

It's an odd charge, since it was Fagan's own company that brought him in for *Dancing*, was there for one of his two coming-out interviews, gave him his only live TV interview between the combine and the draft, promoted him with their ESPY Award, then did an entire segment on his showering habits with the Rams.

In reality, none of these things distracted Sam from making the Rams or Alouettes rosters or staying on the teams. Not one. None of them kept him from a single workout or study session. Believe it or not, even gay athletes are able to tackle and chew gum at the same time. (Funny how we never hear this "distraction" criticism of straight athletes who fill plenty of media requests and endorsement obligations.) Yet the media continued to make blatantly untrue claims—"The team of advisors around him jumped at every contract placed in front of them"—misplacing blame on some mythical "media distractions" that allegedly derailed Sam's career.

While Fagan herself is an out lesbian and a powerful advocate for LGBT people in sports, I had King pegged as a homophobe for the way he treated Sam publicly.

I had read him wrong.

Three days before Super Bowl XLIX, I was at the Seattle Seahawks' last media day before the game. I sat at a table waiting for defensive line coach Travis Jones. I wanted to talk with him about Sam for a lengthy column I would eventually write about the reasons the defensive end wasn't in the league.

At the table next to me sat King, alone, shuffling through

some papers. I hemmed and hawed about whether to say hello, but I was working on this column about the one-year anniversary of Sam coming out. Talking to King, who had the ear of every NFL executive, would be a big boost to the piece and I knew he could offer some insight. Even if he was homophobic.

So I went and said hello. He couldn't have been more gracious, setting down his stack of papers to catch up. We had talked at length at the NFL Annual Meeting ten months earlier. We had, no doubt, read each other's work since then.

As we talked about Sam and gay issues in sports, I sensed something odd coming from King. He felt uncomfortable talking to me, like there was something he wanted to say but didn't know how. After a few minutes it finally came out.

"My daughter's getting married in California this May," he said.

What a nonsequitor. Great, why do I care?

"And for us, we couldn't be more happy than to have her fiancée Kim become part of the family."

Kim is not a Korean man.

But I am most definitely an asshole.

This father, who has the ears of so many other fathers in this country, who is one of the main connections between them and their great love of the NFL, had seemingly struggled the way my father had with his gay child. And he had come out on the same end of it as my father had, loving his lesbian daughter and, maybe even more importantly, fully embracing her partner.

I had done the same thing to Peter King that so many sports writers had done to macho, straight pro athletes for so many years: I assumed the worst. All along King had been trying to stay objective, keeping at bay (he told me) his personal hopes that Sam would make it in the NFL. He had been letting the facts speak for themselves instead of commenting on them.

I implored King to write about his daughter. She had been reticent to let him do so. Yet he and I knew the power his words would have in the ongoing march toward equality. In the spring of 2015, King finally got to share all of his pride for his daughter and her beautiful new wife in a powerful column for *Sports Illustrated*. In its own way, the King family had finally been able to "come out" publicly.

You never know what writer, coach, or athlete has been personally, deeply affected by these issues.

# 11

## "He Might Be a Fag, but He's Our Fag"

*It's Super Bowl 51,* or LI, or whatever the NFL decides to go with for the 2016 season. Michael Sam has fought his way through a season in the Canadian Football League, two training camps, and three practice squads. He was picked up by the Carolina Panthers earlier in the season and cracked the active roster. Now he's on the field for the Super Bowl. What a difference two years make.

Late in the game, the New England Patriots are driving. It's going to be Tom Brady's last season with the Patriots, and they are trailing by five points with a minute left. Brady's chance to ride off just like John Elway, at the very apex of the NFL, hinges on this drive. The Panthers are looking for their first Super Bowl title—playing the team and the quarterback who beat them the last time they were there.

It doesn't get better than this.

It's 3rd and 8 at the Panthers' twenty yard line with forty seconds left. The Patriots have used all their timeouts just to climb back into this game they once trailed by twelve. Brady drops back to pass and Sam comes off the edge. The secondary has the Patriots receivers blanketed on the short routes. Brady steps up into the pocket to buy more time. Sam puts a move on the right tackle and breaks free, reaching for Brady's arm as he winds up for a pass into the end zone . . .

Fumble! The ball is on the ground! Sam rolls off of Brady

onto the ball, wrapping his entire body around the game-winner. There's a pile-up as the Patriots now fight for their championship lives in the scrum. As the officials pull off the players in the following minute, Sam comes up with the ball—he has iced the Super Bowl for the Panthers.

Now, the question.

Are there any Panthers fans from Asheville to Wilmington who could possibly care—in that moment—that Sam is gay? Is there a single Panthers fan in Houston's NRG Stadium who jumps out of his seat and screams, "Oh no, not the gay guy!" On the opposite side of the field, is there a single Patriots fan who is concerned that it was Sam, not another Panthers defensive lineman, who ruined their team's chance of an historic Super Bowl win?

Not. A. Chance.

At Super Bowl XLIX, I proactively searched for a Patriots or Seahawks fan who would find a problem with having an openly gay man playing for her team on the eve of the Super Bowl. So as not to bias any answers, I didn't reveal for whom I was writing, that I was gay, or even my name. I also dressed as conservatively as possible—I left my Nike rainbow #BeTrue shoes in the hotel that day. I asked random strangers wearing Marshawn Lynch jerseys in the street. I talked to the people in line at the coffee house. I grabbed families at the hotel bar and in the NFL Fan Experience. I asked them all, "Would you have any problem if one of the players on your team was gay?"

Every single one of the dozens of people I spoke to said, "No way," many of them excited to share their personal feelings of support for a possible gay player. For fans in Phoenix at the Super Bowl—there to watch their team play in the biggest game of the year—a gay Seahawk or Patriot was the last thing on their mind. They couldn't care less if their team had someone with six arms and horns growing out of his head.

Yet these are the people so many in sports tell us are the problem: the fans are the reason gay athletes won't come out in the pros. They'll stop buying season tickets, they won't purchase jerseys, they'll yell out so much homophobia during practices and games that it will make the gay athlete's experience a living hell.

All of it, every last assertion about the fans in America, is utter bullshit.

In late 2010, George Washington University women's basketball player Kye Allums became the NCAA's first Division I out transgender athlete. While Allums transitioned from female to male during his junior season with the team, he had already adopted what might be described as "more masculine" attire. Dresses and skirts and blouses were nowhere to be found; backward baseball caps and baggy pants were his daily apparel even before he transitioned to male.

When I wrote his coming-out story—that ultimately became a national sensation—I asked him about the fans. We're told one of the factors keeping athletes in the closet is the fear of opposing fans raining down horrific comments.

"I love it," Allums said of fans who hurled comments about him being a man. "I say, *Yeah, you're right.* It makes me feel better about myself to hear them call me a man."

What people assumed to be a negative, Allums took as positive reinforcement. He was a man, even though the fans didn't know it, so the attempted name-calling was affirmation of his true self.

Other gay athletes I've spoken to have returned the incredibly rare "faggot" comments they've heard with an affirmative, "Yeah, so what?"

LGBT athletes in the closet have already heard it all. They've heard the fans boo, they've heard the epithets, they've seen the signs held up in the arena. They've heard it from their teammates, they've heard it from the opposing teams, they've heard it during games, they've seen it on social media.

Brooke Wilson knew all that before Allums's story hit the national media. She wasn't worried. Wilson, one of Allums's GWU teammates, had no fear of the fans' reactions to Allums coming out. She didn't expect to hear anything the team hadn't already had to handle.

"They say things about me, they say things about Coach, they say things about everybody," Wilson said. "We've been through it all."

While there are trickles of homophobia in the stands of American sports, the preponderance of homophobic comments from sports fans at American sporting events, as I've said, is blown way out of proportion. Perception doesn't meet reality, particularly in professional sports. While a snide comment here and there certainly makes its way out of the stands, or a group of drunk knuckleheads at a college basketball game might get out of hand with a poorly worded chant, they are few and far between.

Many sports institutions, from professional leagues to college conferences to the NCAA itself, have created fan-conduct policies that specifically forbid homophobic chants or comments (along with the banning of comments based on gender, race, and other demographics). The University of Richmond, for example, has laid it out in black and white: "Derogatory comments directed toward officials, student-athletes, coaches, team representatives, university employees and fans regarding race, religion, sexual orientation, gender, gender identity, gender expression as well as national or ethnic origin will not be tolerated."

It doesn't get more clear and comprehensive than that. Many schools have these policies posted around their stadiums and arenas, some of them even reading it over the loudspeaker before games. College-age sports fans can certainly be creative and effective with their in-game chants and distractions. And, as witnessed by Allums in 2010, some can cross the line. Yet few twenty-year-old college students want to risk losing their season tickets by spewing homophobia at an opposing shooting guard; there are many other equally effective ways of getting under their skin. Just ask the Cameron Crazies.

Even with these policies, the lack of homophobic and transphobic chanting at sporting events is largely self-regulating. Without threats by schools, most sports fans these days simply don't want to cross that line for the same reason many athletes have changed their tunes about having gay teammates: more and more of them have brothers and aunts and college roommates who have come out to them. If they wouldn't say it in front of the people they care about, they won't say it in front of a crowd of people in an arena.

Evan Risk is a junior high school cross-country coach near Iowa City. Risk is a devout Iowa Hawkeyes fan, attending as many men's basketball games as his schedule allows. During a game of the 2013–14 season, one of Risk's buddies told him he had taken a popular Hawkeyes postgame chant about beer and rewritten the words: *"In heaven there are no queers, that's why we kill them here, and when we're gone from here, our friends will be killing all the queers."*

Risk is gay, but his friend was unaware. Risk debated internally for days about coming out to his friend. He simply didn't want to hear the chant again, so he got the courage to tell his friend. He told him what that chant meant to him when he heard it. The friend was devastated that he had hurt Risk. He wouldn't let it happen again.

A couple weeks later they were again at a Hawkeyes game with some friends. During a timeout someone's roommate hollered at the opposing team, "That's so fucking gay!" Risk didn't have to do a thing. "Don't say that," his friend said. "Don't use that word that way."

Only weeks before, the kid had been chanting about *"killing all the queers."* Immediately after his friend came out to him, he was telling other people to stop doing that very thing.

We've seen the acceptance of gay athletes by fans for years.

No matter what poll you look at, or how you slice and dice the demographics, the vast majority of Americans have no problem with gay athletes. One of the latest polls, conducted in early 2015 by the Public Religion Research Institute, found only 19 percent of Americans would oppose a professional sports team (not their favorite, but the undefined "any") signing a gay or lesbian player. Almost three-quarters, 73 percent, said they supported the idea. That's about the same number we've seen in polls like this for the better part of a decade. For context on the significance of that 73 percent, it might be helpful to know that:

- the same number of Americans—73 percent—believe Jesus was born to a virgin, and a full 74 percent believe an angel appeared in a field shortly after he was born and told some shepherds about it;
- a 2014 poll found that only 74 percent of Americans agree that the earth revolves around the sun, and 26 percent—more than oppose gay athletes—believe the sun revolves around the earth;
- the same poll also found that only 48 percent of Americans agree that humans evolved from another species.

So 73 percent agreement on the acceptance of gay athletes is just about as good as it gets.

Despite the numbers and the lack of concrete examples of fans mistreating gay athletes, some outspoken power brokers in sports still believe fans are the reason we don't have more out gay professional athletes.

"I don't think the locker room would have any problem with it," Arizona Cardinals head coach Bruce Arians said about having a gay player in the NFL. This was before Michael Sam had come out, when the idea was simply a fantasy. "The problem would be with the fans. I think especially opposing fans. Some of the things that are said are over the top and out of control that I can imagine what some fans would say to an openly gay player."

While Arians and others can certainly have their opinions of fans, a poll taken just a couple weeks before his public comments in 2013 told the real story. Turnkey Sports and Entertainment, a search firm for sports executives in college and the pros, found that 85 percent of sports executives think fans are indifferent to whether a team signs an openly gay player.

Even that 85 percent may be underestimating fans. Certainly there is a battalion of tweeters and Internet commenters who jump on every story about a gay athlete and declare, "I don't care." Yet even opposing fans have extended a warm welcome to gay athletes on the visiting team.

Jason Collins took the court for the Brooklyn Nets as an openly gay man for the first time on February 23, 2014. It was an away game against the Los Angeles Lakers. Collins received applause, some people standing. He didn't hear a single epithet. I can hear the "of course there wouldn't be an issue in Hollywood" excuses. In the next week Collins had the same experience in Portland and Denver.

*Sure, that's the crazy West Coast,* the doubters will claim. *Everybody's a little gay out there.*

Michael Sam's first preseason road game was at the Cleveland

Browns. Sam got polite applause there too. In blue-collar Cleveland. At the Dawg Pound. That's not to mention the raucus cheers he received at the NFL draft from New York Jets fans (who booed just about every other pick).

Robbie Rogers has now played three full seasons in Major League Soccer. He hasn't had a single incident with any comments from any fans during any road game. Same with UMass–turned–Seton Hall guard Derrick Gordon.

As Risk's story illustrates, when people know a gay person is within earshot they are far less likely to use that kind of language. The fans are not an issue.

Even if the fans did say something homophobic, gay athletes can take it in stride like Allums. Collins revealed that one NBA player made a nasty comment to him during a Nets game in 2014. Collins laughed it off as being the foolish thoughts of "one knucklehead from another team," he told the *New York Daily News*. "He's a knucklehead. So I just let it go."

Incidentally, Arians revealed to me at Super Box XLIX that he had been considering signing Sam to the Cardinals. It seems even Arians has learned the error of his thinking.

Outside of North America, this is a completely different issue.

While fans of North American teams, from the Maple Leafs to the Marlins, the Patriots to the Padres, certainly take their sports seriously, they don't hold a candle to soccer fans in South America, Europe, and Africa. Religion plays a big role in sports here in the United States, yet sports *are* religion in some other parts of the world.

That passion for sports—and soccer in particular—around the rest of the globe translates into the most vicious behavior by fans, and that manifests itself in routine displays of public homophobia at soccer matches.

One team in UK soccer has had it particularly bad. Brighton & Hove Albion is a Football League Championship team that plays along the southern coast of England. Brighton & Hove is known for its strong LGBT population, reflected in a 2011 census that showed the area had the most dense population of same-sex civil partnerships in the country. Brighton & Hove is England's San Francisco.

For years, opposing fans have pummeled the players and supporters of Brighton & Hove with the most vile homophobia. In 2013 the club's supporters put together a report chronicling the abuse the team had witnessed over the previous season. It was eye-popping. A lengthy list of all the chants heard from opposing fans reflected abuse in 57 percent of the team's games—often multiple times during games—that season. The chants included:

- *"Town full of faggots"*
- *"Palace 5, Brighton none, Brighton take it up the bum"*
- *"Go home, you qayers"*
- *"Up your arse, up your arse, if you're not a fucking wanker you're a qayer"*
- *"We drink cider, you suck cock"*

Their report of a September 2012 game at Burnley offered this description of fan behavior: "Home fans used many derogative words. So bad that BBC Sussex radio had to turn off a microphone and apologize several times on air for the language being used around them."

Lovely.

The most common chant heard by the Brighton & Hove supporters was simply, *"We can see you holding hands."* It's seemingly innocuous enough—people hold hands all the time, straight couples, gay couples. No big deal. Yet in the context of the abuse at more than half of the club's games, and the insidious nature of so many of the comments and chants heard by opposing fans, that simple chant takes on a powerfully destructive meaning. The fact that it was heard by observers at a dozen of the team's matches that season indicates the copycat mentality of ill-intentioned fans.

Mind you, this is just one—though likely the most overwhelming—example of the homophobic actions of English soccer fans.

Homophobic abuse has been so rampant throughout the Premiere League and lower levels of soccer that it has gone beyond the purview of the Football Association—the Crown Prosecution Service itself, which is headed up by Great Britain's attorney general, is taking criminal action against fans who use homophobic and racist chants during matches, or who use racist or homophobic bullying tactics online against fans or players. Fans can be banned from attending games if found guilty, and in 2014 those fans who had been found guilty were banned from attending the World Cup in Brazil.

Racism, in addition to homophobia, has long been a black eye for the fans of soccer across Europe. Fans continue to throw bananas onto soccer pitches in Europe as a way to taunt black players, in effect calling them monkeys. When a banana landed in front of Brazilian player Dani Alves during a Spanish soccer match in 2014, he bent down, peeled the banana, and ate it. That prompted soccer players around the world, including Brazil's Neymar and Belgium's Dries Mertens, to post pictures of themselves eating bananas on social media in support of Alves.

Players are fighting back against the fans' homophobia as well. In 2013, the United Kingdom's largest LGBT-rights group, Stonewall, created a rainbow-laces campaign. While players cannot alter their uniforms—jerseys or shorts or shoes—to demonstrate support of various companies or causes, Stonewall got creative by shipping English professional soccer players rainbow-colored laces they could put into their shoes (with the approval of the Premiere League, of course). In 2014, players from seventy different professional football clubs, including Premiere League teams like Arsenal, wore the special rainbow laces.

This dynamic came to an international head at the 2014 World Cup. During the goal kicks of opponents' goalies, Mexico fans would chant *"puto"*—a gay slur that translates literally as "male prostitute." When *Outsports* raised the issue during the World Cup, some Mexico fans jumped to their defense saying that they weren't attacking anyone's sexual orientation, they were simply trying to insult the other team . . . by, of course, calling them gay.

It harkens back to the "Kobe Bryant defense," in which calling someone "faggot" isn't supposed to be offensive to gay people. Yet when you use a racial or sexist or homophobic slur to denigrate someone else, you're reinforcing the idea that the offended group is "less than." That was a concept that escaped Mexico fans, who decided to not just continue the practice, but to expand its use to all kicks by the opposing team during the World Cup.

While English soccer has deemed the practice actionable and has punished fans for it—in the stadium and in the courts—FIFA decided that it was perfectly fine, blessing the homophobic chant of Mexico fans.

International soccer still has a long way to go.

To Americans, the behavior of so many international soccer fans is incomprehensible. While acceptance of same-sex marriage is more widespread in Britain than it is in the United States—in early 2014 it had about 68 percent acceptance in Britain compared to about 50 percent in the US—the acceptance of homophobic abuse by fans is also strangely more accepted.

It's impossible to imagine the fans at Heinz Field or Mile High Stadium breaking into chants mocking the race or sexual orientation of anyone in the stadium, be they players, coaches, or fans.

Yet that's exactly what people like Arians have put forward: American football fans will suddenly devolve into English football fans if a gay athlete takes the field. They will rain down so much homophobia on the player and his team that it will become impossible to function, a distraction that eats at the core of a gay player and his team. Doubters look at the reception Jackie Robinson received from many white fans in 1947 and project that hatred onto straight sports fans of today.

It's simply not true. Collins hasn't experienced it. Sam hasn't heard it. Rogers hasn't felt it. Many other male athletes in high school and college have shared the same sentiment: the fans simply don't use sexual orientation or homophobic slurs to demean opponents nearly as much as you may think.

The misperception comes from something buried in us after so many years of hearing from people in power—ministers, politicians, teachers, parents, high school bullies—that being gay is wrong. While most of America has come to not just tolerate but accept people for being gay, we are still convinced that others have not.

One of the very early polls on this subject laid it out perfectly. In 2005, *Sports Illustrated* talked to fans about their acceptance of gay athletes and their perception of the issue. A decade ago, 78 percent of those polled said it was okay to them for gay athletes to participate in sports. That was two years before John Amaechi came out, nine years before Jason Collins took the court as an out gay man. Same-sex marriage was legal in only one state: Massachusetts. Yet over three-quarters of the people in the *Sports Illustrated* poll said sports should be open to gay people.

Still, almost the same number—68 percent—in the same

poll said they believed that coming out would hurt an athlete's professional career.

In 2005, the personal acceptance of gay athletes by fans was already there. People had turned a corner, a result of the death of Matthew Shepard, the coming-out of people like Corey Johnson and Esera Tuaolo, and all the other events that had come before them. Yet there was still the dominant idea that gays were not generally accepted, as reflected by the lack of equal rights. Heck, three years later, none of the leading Democratic candidates for president of the United States supported same-sex marriage rights. It's understandable.

The disconnect was a result of the conflation of the acceptance of same-sex marriage and the acceptance of gay people simply kicking a ball around. Despite the lagging of the public to go full-equality with the LGBT community and grant equal legal recognition of their relationships, there simply wasn't a reticence to support them playing the sport they love and doing their job.

Ten years later, of course, the conversation about same-sex marriage transformed when the Supreme Court brought marriage equality to LGBT people in this country. In 2015 polls showed about 60 percent of Americans supported the rights of gay couples to marry. Yet even with that support—overwhelming compared to where that number was a decade before—people still believe a fan would care if their team had a gay guy in the showers with his teammates. The majority of fans still think, *I'm not homophobic . . . but the guy next to me is.* The thing is, the guy next to them is saying the same thing. And the woman next to him.

If they simply talked with one another it would become crystal clear very quickly: homophobia amongst American sports fans is dead.

 *Fallon Fox Is the Bravest Athlete in History*

***From the first time I spoke with her,*** I have known no one in sports more brave than Fallon Fox.

While the two words are often conflated, "brave" is actually the opposite of "fearless." Fearlessness takes no bravery. If there's no fear, an athlete doesn't have to dig deep to find herself, to find the strength it will take to overcome whatever obstacle she faces. There's no fear to overcome; she's just not afraid of it. Bravery is acting in the *presence* of fear.

The biggest fear many LGBT athletes face is simply the fear in their own heads. The imagined reaction of people is many times worse than the embrace that often greets them when they come out. Fox had seen and heard many of the same anti-gay, anti-trans things so many LGBT athletes have heard around the locker rooms and gyms. Like so many before her, she knew that when she came out she would face a torrent of backlash from fans and athletes in her sport. While those fears usually go unrealized, in Fox's case, she was right. The source of the fear she faced was very real.

In my first conversation with her, in March of 2013, she was desperately scared. She had been fighting in women's MMA for a couple years, most recently as a professional fighter. She was good. Not great yet, but good. She was a bit older than most of her competitors and that proved to be a disadvantage. At her last fight before I heard from her, a reporter had been snooping around and discovered that Fox is transgender. The reporter's plan was allegedly to out her publicly in a few days, whether she was ready or not. She wasn't ready. Neither was her sport.

When she found her way to me, Fox was scared that her boxing license would be revoked if the Florida State Boxing Commission learned she was trans. She was scared that women would refuse to fight her. She was scared that promoters wouldn't give her fights. She was scared of losing the one thing that had become a constant refuge while she battled the fear building inside her as she transitioned genders: the sport of mixed martial arts.

The best way to tackle the fear of being outed is to come out by telling your story your way. Michael Sam jumped ahead of reporters asking invasive questions at the Pro Bowl. Actor Neil Patrick Harris shared his truth with *People* magazine when a rash of rumors and speculation hit the Internet. Fox was no different, sharing her story as a transgender fighter with both *Sports Illustrated* and me at *Outsports*. It was a big deal. Very few trans athletes had come out publicly, let alone in such an explosive sport like MMA. Yet amidst the fear of losing everything, Fox stepped out into the light.

I've seen a lot of athletes come out at every level of sports. High school football, college tennis, professional basketball. Never have I seen anything like the reaction Fox faced from people in mixed martial arts. The basis for her fear became present like no athlete in my professional career.

The venom over Fox's participation in women's MMA wasn't about the rights of trans people. Her very existence in the sport became about one simple response: anger.

"You're a fucking man," MMA commentator Joe Rogan said just about as pleasantly as he's capable. "That's a man, okay? I don't care if you don't have a dick anymore."

"That is a lying, sick, sociopathic, disgusting freak," MMA fighter Matt Mitrione preached. "And I mean that. Because you lied on your license to beat up women. That's disgusting."

The "lied on your license" piece stemmed from Fox claiming she was female (she was, though many in MMA simply won't accept that) and not sharing that she had sex-reassignment surgery. (Given the reaction, you might understand why that slipped her mind.)

The comments on top MMA blogs like *Bloody Elbow* went wild, something out of a horror flick. Anonymous fans couldn't wait to descend on the Internet to spew the most venomous bile they could dream up while looming over their keyboards. Site moderators were working overtime.

Fox's license was put on a kind of administrative hold as the Florida State Boxing Commission investigated the situation. Though they quickly cleared up the issue and gave Fox the green light, she struggled to find matches—fighters willing to step into the ring with her—once the tournament she had been involved with ended.

The refusal of many women to fight Fox, and the rejection of the idea by promoters, has been based on one key assumption: men are dangerous to women.

The battle over trans inclusion in other sports has revolved for the most part around the idea of "fairness." One athlete should not have an "unfair" advantage over any other athlete. It's why performance-enhancing drugs have come under such scrutiny in recent years. People want athletes on a level playing field and something like drugs are outside that realm.

Except, the entire premise of "fairness" in our binary sports world is a lie.

Reggie Miller is one of the greatest NBA players of all time.

The 6'7" guard for the Indiana Pacers was an assassin on the court, shooting daggers from three-point range while racking up five NBA All-Star appearances and 25,000 career points. His sister, Cheryl Miller, was one of the greatest female basketball players of all time, winning an Olympic gold in 1984 and being inducted into the Basketball Hall of Fame. Cheryl was 6'2", 180 pounds.

I'm 6'2", 175 pounds. Yet simply because her gender is female, Cheryl competed against women, while I have to compete against her 6'7" brother. Not only does Reggie have a 5" advantage over me, he had a quickness I simply don't have (and I'm not slow).

For some reason, Reggie's advantages over me are deemed "fair." Yet if I tried to compete against women like Cheryl, my nonexistent advantages over her would be deemed "unfair" simply because I am a man. Even with all of my "unfair advantages," Cheryl would wipe the court with me. I'm left to compete against men like Kobe Bryant, Shaquille O'Neal, and Michael Jordan. Again, how are their advantages over me deemed "fair" yet I am deemed to have "unfair" advantages over Cheryl Miller, with her Hall of Fame status and gold medals? Or Brittney Griner, with her seven foot–plus wing span?

To be sure, the fastest man in the world can run the 100-meter dash in less time than the fastest woman. The strongest man can hurl the shot put farther than the strongest woman. More NBA players can dunk the ball than can WNBA players.

Yet the vast majority of men are slower and weaker than the fastest and strongest women. We ignore the fact that our gender does not define our excellence in sports. At a very young age we force the boys to play with the boys and the girls to play with the girls. We tell them that the boys are inherently more athletic, more capable of scoring goals and shooting baskets. At some age, to some extent, this becomes increasingly true. Yet Brittney Griner can dominate almost any man in a game of one-on-one. How many men have any advantage—"fair" or "unfair"—over Griner? One percent? Two percent?

Why did we decide that we would divide sports participation by gender? Why not strength? Why not speed? Why not height or weight?

Decades ago, women were strongly discouraged from playing sports altogether. There was no "women's league" because women simply didn't play basketball or soccer. On the other hand, women have been competing in tennis and golf for over a century. These sports were deemed safe for women to play. They didn't involve person-to-person contact and they would be played in skirts. Yet even in 1948, Babe Zaharias, one of the greatest female athletes of the twentieth century, was denied the right to play in the US Open because it was "only for men." The US Women's Open was only three years old at the time and Zaharias wanted some stiffer competition. Rejected by the men, she competed against the women. She won.

Women at the time were barred from competing in any kind of long-distance race, forget about a marathon. The belief was that any distance over 2.5 miles was dangerous for women as the pavement-pounding could make them infertile. I kid you not. It wasn't until the late sixties, when several women crashed the Boston Marathon that marathons began to allow female registrants. One of those brave pioneers, incidentally, was Patricia Nell Warren, who went on to write *The Front Runner*, one of the best-selling gay-themed novels of all time, about a distance runner in the Olympics. Without her participation in those marathons, millions of gay athletes would not have been inspired by that book.

Barring women from playing sports seems like a severe case of insanity today. Yet it's the same mentality that drove the division of sports to be based on gender rather than ability. Our sports, from high school to the NCAA to professional leagues, carry with us the legacy of a time when women were deemed unworthy of the title "athlete."

The biases we levy against trans athletes are no different. Instead of focusing on skill and excellence, we focus on sexual organs. The only thing that matters to our system in determining competition is whether someone was born with testicles or not. That's what it comes down to: two sacks of skin hanging between somebody's legs. If you have them at birth, you're in one category. If you don't, you're in another "lesser" category. Nothing else—race, height, weight, mental capacity—matters at all.

Trans people don't associate with their assigned gender at birth. Because they reject the gender they were assigned at birth, "that's their problem." "Deal with it." Sounds harsh, but that is the world of sports.

We heard a lot of this echoed when ESPN announced it would give its annual Arthur Ashe Courage Award to Caitlyn Jenner. The torrent of attacks came from across traditional and social media, claiming Jenner wasn't courageous enough for the award. Surely there had to be others who were more brave, as though we can compare the levels of courage two people display when they act in the face of fear.

"I'm pretty sure they could've found someone—and this is not anything against Caitlyn Jenner—who was much closer actively involved in sports, who would've been deserving of what that award represents," commentator Bob Costas said.

*Not anything against Caitlyn Jenner.* Bullshit.

Costas did not say raise this issue in 2009 when ESPN gave the award to Nelson Mandela, who had never participated in elite sports and hadn't played a sport at any level in decades. He didn't object in 2008 when they gave the award to the "black fist" sprinters, John Carlos and Tommie Smith, who last competed in the Olympics in 1968. When the award went to the four passengers who took down United flight 93 on September 11, 2001, thereby sabotaging the hijackers' plans for the plane, Costas didn't have a problem then.

Instead, he reserved his judgment for a trans woman who had once been the greatest male athlete in the world, and who would open a worldwide conversation about trans issues. Somehow that person—in the eyes of Costas and so many others—was undeserving.

Putting aside the argument of whether any advantage is "unfair," the individuals and organizations who have done the research on trans athletes and hormones have all come to the same conclusion: trans athletes who have completed a full physical transition should be free to compete as their declared gender. Any advantages that linger are . . . "fair."

In 2003, the International Olympic Committee created a trans-specific policy that opened the door for participation if an athlete underwent sex-reassignment surgery, had hormone treatments for at least two years, and received legal recognition of their transitioned sex. One, two, three. If a trans athlete executed those three steps, she could freely compete as a female athlete. While some claim that combat sports need stricter guidelines due to "safety" issues, the Olympics host women's competitions in boxing, judo, and tae kwon do.

Even with those combat sports, some claim that MMA and professional boxing present another class of safety issues. That's why the Association of Boxing Commissions put together their own transsexual policy. If a male-to-female individual physically transitions before puberty, she is automatically considered female. No questions asked. If someone transitions after puberty, there's a separate policy that looks almost identical to the IOC policy:

sex-reassignment surgery, two years of hormones, and a letter from a board-certified physician.

For the record, Fox had sex-reassignment surgery six years before fighting professionally and had been taking hormones for ten years. Despite hormone treatment five times longer than what the ABC required, doubters continue to attack Fox to this day. While the Florida State Boxing Commission took up the issue of Fox's license shortly after she came out publicly, her license was never suspended or revoked.

There have been many other elite-level sports organizations that have adopted paths to participation for trans athletes. In 2010 the Ladies Professional Golf Association members voted to discontinue the tour's policy that competitors had to be biologically "female at birth." Various sports—including USA Boxing and USA Track & Field—have adopted the IOC's policy. The NCAA's policy is one of the most inclusive, mandating no required surgery and only one year of testosterone-suppression treatment before competing in women's sports. NIRSA, which oversees intramural sports on college campuses, goes even further, allowing trans athletes to compete as their expressed gender without any medical treatment, focusing on themes of empowerment and inclusion.

The ABC's policy is particularly interesting because it talks about prepuberty transitions as being no issue. It's why so many trans advocates have pushed for K–12 sports to allow trans participation in the same vein as NIRSA: simply based on gender expression. The ABC policy certainly affirms that goal through the time when most athletes are in junior high school. Once puberty hits for tweens, the surge of testosterone in boys gives them that sudden "unfair advantage," according to the mantra.

At the core of the discussion is the purpose of high school sports. At the professional level, the goal is to win. Certainly there's an inspirational aspect to professional sports. Community-building and role-modeling all play into it. But at the end of the match, the goal is to win. You get paid more if you perform well; you get paid less if you don't.

The goals of scholastic sports are much more complex. The role of education—to teach athletes the values of hard work, determination, and inclusion—is paramount to coaching student-athletes. Giving those athletes life skills that they will carry into adulthood is crucial to the success of coaches and high school sports programs. Winning is a bonus, a byproduct of good instruction.

Allowing trans athletes in K–12 sports to participate as their expressed gender makes all the sense in the world. Requiring teenagers to go through sex-reassignment surgery or block their natural production of testosterone is a lot to ask. Many teenagers today experiment with different gender expression, just as some of them experiment with sex with partners of the same gender. In order to find one's true self, a trans-female teenager may want to participate in girls' sports as a way of exploring her identity.

More than half of all trans youth attempt suicide before their twentieth birthday. Why would we make it even more difficult for them to find their place in our society? Why would we not open every door possible for them and make them feel like they belong wherever they feel they need to be?

Arguments about advantages and disadvantages, winning and losing, take a backseat to the physical and psychological well-being of these youth who simply want to express their true selves on the court.

What's particularly revealing about the controversy over Fallon Fox is the design of mixed martial arts and other combat sports. Fox is placed into a category based on her weight so she only competes against other women her size. This isn't Rob Gronkowski stepping into the ring with Tara Lipinski. This is two people of similar height, similar weight, and similar strength competing against one another.

Even with the designed control of all of these variables, the mixed martial arts world has collectively banished Fox. They have come up with a rationalization that her bone density is higher than that of her cisgender competitors because she was born male. They have mounted an entire campaign against Fox based on this bone density argument.

Yet I have never heard anyone who believes bone density should be a consideration when determining fighting class. No one is talking about dividing fighters based on their bone density. Just as testosterone levels vary widely from woman to woman and man to man, bone density is not a constant among people. It's only when it comes to Fox and other trans fighters that this suddenly becomes an important factor in determining fairness.

There is also no discussion about the fact that bone density varies between people of different races. Clinical studies from the 1950s to today all say the same thing: black people on average have a higher bone density than whites. One study published in the *American Journal of Public Health* in 2007 showed that white people are twice as likely to break their hips as black people. In fact, a black woman is less likely to break her hip than a white man. Is that ever raised as a necessary variable when determining fairness? Never.

In addition to bone density, the very makeup of Fox's muscles have been called into question. Because Fox was "born a man," she must have more "muscle mass," and that equals an unfair advantage (even though the sport is already equalized based on weight). A recent episode of *Sports Science* took up this topic and showed that Lucia Rijker, a Dutch professional female boxer, was able to generate more force with her muscles (922 pounds of force) than

Manny Pacquiao (810). And Rijker weighs less than Pacquiao.

The bone density argument? Irrelevant. The muscle mass argument? Not true. Yet Fox continues to be rejected for fights by promoters and other fighters. The UFC has said she won't be fighting women under their banner.

It is baseless transphobia. Period.

These same transphobic apologists say this alleged bone density and muscle mass make Fox a physical threat to other fighters. Think about that. These fighters step into a ring together wearing virtually no protective gear, governed by a set of rules barring very few fighting tactics. They are in the ring trying to knock their opponents unconscious, break noses, or otherwise leave them incapacitated. Yet when it comes to a trans fighter simply stepping into the ring to fight, "safety" suddenly becomes a pressing concern.

Fox has competed in five professional matches. She has never broken the bone of an opponent. She has never knocked another opponent unconscious. In fact, she hasn't even won all of her matches. She lost to a woman named Ashlee Evans-Smith. It wasn't much of a fight. Evans-Smith dominated Fox for most of the match and took her out in the third round. Pro MMA fighter John Dodson summed it up perfectly: "Wow, I just watched Fallon Fox get destroyed by Ashlee Evans-Smith."

Yet even after Fox was "destroyed," many of these same people claimed her advantages were unfair. Evans-Smith was one of them. After claiming victory over Fox, Evans-Smith said, "I don't feel like she should fight women. I feel like there should be a unique organization for those needs. She did have an advantage. She definitely did." A year later, Evans-Smith was suspended from competition. She had used a banned substance. She had cheated. Yet to her, Fox was the athlete who deserved expulsion.

The most revealing reaction may be that of Ronda Rousey, the most well-known and highly decorated female MMA fighter.

Rousey said she would refuse to fight Fox or any trans fighter. In all likelihood, Rousey would clobber Fox as she's a technically better and more experienced fighter.

"Unfair advantages" are simply code words for "transphobia."

Naysayers might have a point if the history of sports had been littered with the domination of MTF trans athletes. It has not.

Renée Richards, the pioneering professional tennis player who in the 1970s sued for the right to play in the US Open, was anything but dominant. In her one Grand Slam singles tournament in Flushing Meadows in 1979, she lost in the third round. She made it to the finals of the US Open doubles tournament where she lost . . . to Martina Navratilova.

Gabrielle Ludwig was a center for the Mission College women's basketball team. At 6'6", Ludwig towered over her opponents. Yet even at the community college level she could not carry her team to a state championship. She blossomed her senior year, averaging twenty rebounds and being named a First-Team All-Conference player. Now she coaches—even her height and frame didn't get her to the next level of sports.

Mianne Bagger is a trans golfer whose professional career has never gotten on track. In 2009 Lana Lawless did win the Long Drivers of America title, but she never won an LPGA Tour event.

No trans MTF athlete has ever dominated her sport. None have ever exhibited unfair advantages that cisgender women have not beaten in competition.

On the flip side there's the phenomenon known as Chris Mosier, an FTM trans triathlete who defies all of the myths about the unfair advantages of trans women over their competitors. Mosier has transitioned from female to male and now races against other men, mostly cisgender men. And he's kicking ass.

Mosier had held back from a hormonal transition for years. He had wanted to see how far he could take his competitive career and was doing well against female competitors. He wasn't winning races, but he was doing well. He figured once he started hormonal treatments and was forced to compete with the men, he would suddenly be a "middle of the pack" triathlete.

Eventually, racing against women didn't feel right anymore. It wasn't a moral argument for him; he was a man and felt he should be racing against the men. He began hormone treatments, registered for the 2011 New York City Triathlon as a male competitor, and talked to the *New York Times* about diving into the race as man for the first time.

That *New York Times* article awakened something in Mosier he didn't see coming. The tone of the article reflected low expectations for him as a male athlete. He'd be running with the big boys now, so good luck placing. Mosier's own comments reflected this as well. Yet it was this dismissive quote from John Korff, the owner of the New York City Triathlon, commenting about Mosier in the *New York Times* that lit a fire in the triathlete: "This is an age grouper who is out to have fun, God bless him," Korff said.

An "age grouper" meant that Mosier was just going out there to run around and have fun, maybe post a personal record and pick up his participation medal. A trans man competing against other men and placing—or crazier yet, winning? Not a chance.

"That didn't sit well with me," Mosier said. "I didn't just want to be an 'age grouper' because I transitioned. I wanted to win."

So he did what all great athletes do to win: He trained. And trained. A dozen times a week, waking up at five a.m., running after work. Within a couple years he was competing, and in 2013 he won the Staten Island Duathlon. He didn't win his age group, he didn't beat the women, he beat *everybody*. Since then he's added age-group wins and other medals. In 2015 Mosier qualified to represent the United States at the ITU Duathlon World Championships as a man.

Part of Mosier's transition has included testosterone treatments. Lest anyone think this might be another form of "unfair advantage," Mosier has—like any trans athlete—received medical use exemptions from the US Anti-Doping Agency and USA Triathlon. His testosterone levels are monitored regularly, including unannounced tests, to ensure those levels are "normal" for his age. "Normal" T levels in men could range anywhere from about 270 ng/dL to 1,070, according to the Mayo Clinic. (The average adult women's range is 15–70.) That very broad range of what is considered "normal" is another example of the desperately inaccurate arguments over unfair advantages.

Rousey said, in her attack on Fox and refusal to fight a trans woman, that if you've gone through puberty with testicles you have an advantage that no one can surpass. That has been one of the drumbeats of the doubters. Yet Mosier is defying that, beating cisgender men in a race of pure talent and skill.

There goes another argument out the window.

Are the issues involving trans athletes all black-and-white? Of course not.

Tennis player Renée Richards, who in the 1970s won the right for trans women to play in the US Open, has thirty years later reconsidered her position on the issue. "Having lived for the past thirty years, I know if I'd had surgery at the age of twenty-two, and then at twenty-four went on the tour, no genetic woman in the world would have been able to come close to me." Richards was in her forties when she transitioned and competed in the US Open.

Ludwig, the 6'6" center, was in her fifties when she competed at Mission College. If she had transitioned and competed in her early twenties, would she have been a dominant center? Maybe. Would she have been better than Brittney Griner? Maybe.

Fox herself didn't fight professionally until her midthirties. If she'd done so a decade earlier, would she have been unstoppable?

Should there be different rules for different ages? Maybe. Most trans advocates understand that there are issues here that need careful consideration, particularly in our binary system of sports. There are key points to be made about testosterone and puberty.

These issues are not black-and-white.

And that's the whole point. We've created a black/white, male/female dichotomy in sports that doesn't reflect the alleged goal of competition: to match people of similar talent and see whose hard work and determination will win the day.

# CONCLUSION
## *Courage Is Contagious*

***I have mentioned the word "fear"*** many dozens of times in this book. For decades fear has been the dominant force determining the lives of LGBT people in sports: fear of retaliation, fear of rejection, fear of exclusion. It's easy for a writer to sit behind his keyboard and lament the LGBT people in sports who have let fear dictate their willingness to live openly and free. I understand that fear on another level.

When I first became a high school football official in Los Angeles, I had various people—mostly gay officials from around the country—tell me not to share my sexual orientation with the other officials. While I had a bit of a national profile, virtually none of these local football officials—mostly blue-collar guys—had any idea who I was. If I wanted to keep my secret, it would be safe.

Like the time I talked with Ahman Green, I knew that couldn't be my path. If I couldn't be my authentic self with my fellow football officials, then who was I to shake my head at other men and women who let fear govern them? I decided I would never shy away from sharing my true self with any of the officials any time I had the opportunity.

It was only a few weeks into my tutelage when that opportunity came along. The administrator for the Los Angeles area, a bigger-than-life guy named Tony Crittendon, asked me after a scrimmage if I could work a game the next day. "I had somebody just cancel on me, so are you free or do you have plans with your wife?"

He had, no doubt, seen my wedding ring and made the assumption for which you could hardly blame him. Truth is, I did have plans with my husband, Dan, the next night. I could have easily laughed it off and politely declined. I didn't.

"You know, Tony, I am married, but I don't have a wife," I said. "I've got a husband. We've been together for ten years." I braced for his reaction, the warnings of other officials in my head.

"That's cool," Tony replied. "So can you work my game?"

I've heard the occasional homophobic remark among my fellow officials over the years, which has only made me more adamant about being open with every single one of them. That led to our unit president addressing homophobia with the officials in 2015 for the first time ever in the unit. Other gay officials have tracked me down for advice and to talk about their experiences. The men who know I'm gay have warmly embraced me virtually every time. One of those men—Al, an African American man in his seventies—has gone out of his way to make sure I feel completely embraced and supported in our LA officials "fraternity." My courage—acting in the face of fear—has had a powerful ripple effect amongst these men.

Yet not everyone finds their way down this path so easily.

Howard Bragman is a big-time publicist in Hollywood. I've mentioned him several times throughout this book because he has played a key role in various athletes coming out, including Sheryl Swoopes, Esera Tuaolo, John Amaechi, and Michael Sam. He has also helped other celebrities come out, like country singer Chely Wright, actress Meredith Baxter, and trans actor and advocate Chaz Bono. Howard's office is located on the outskirts of West Hollywood, the "gayest" neighborhood in Los Angeles. Howard himself is gay.

Yet several years ago, Howard had a closeted gay employee who wouldn't come out to him. Working for a gay publicist in a gay industry helping gay people come out as gay in the gayest neighborhood in a gay industry, this guy still didn't feel comfortable being his authentic self.

Fear is often irrational, and it is the only thing holding us back from true equality in sports.

Fear crushed Saunders High School basketball coach Anthony Nicodemo for many years. When he first contacted me in 2011—completely anonymously, afraid I might reveal his dreaded secret—he was convinced he would never be able to come out to anyone in the world. Working with teenage boys, he thought—he knew—that his career would be over, that parents would refuse to allow their boys to be coached by someone who they might see as a "pedophile." From a traditional New York Italian family, he knew he would be disowned and left alone and unemployed. Anthony was depressed, unhappy, and 350 pounds.

Two years later, Anthony attended the LGBT Sports Summit at Nike World Headquarters in Beaverton, Oregon. There he met a hundred LGBT people in sports—athletes, coaches, activists— who had found their way out of the closet. He made new friends and was suddenly immersed in a community of support.

One of those people was Kirk Walker, a softball coach who had found success at Oregon State after becoming one of the very first publicly out Division I head coaches, and who got a job at UCLA even after coming out. Kirk represented immense possibility to Anthony: being a successful gay coach did not mandate staying in the closet.

A week later, Anthony came out publicly in an article I wrote for *Outsports*. His school administration supported him both privately and publicly. Coaches he had worked with years before contacted him with congratulations for finding the strength to be himself. Closeted coaches and athletes reached out for his help. His family struggled a bit, but they came around.

Most importantly, he didn't lose a single player. The parents didn't fear him, they embraced him and the job he was doing with their sons, some of them praising him in the media. His coaching attracted new players coming to his school from all across Yonkers, looking to play for the coach who had found a way to turn a losing program into a winning team—they couldn't care less that he was gay.

Anthony began working with local LGBT nonprofit groups to build inclusion in Yonkers. He helped to expand a gay-straight alliance at his school. He brought LGBT sensitivity training to his area, working with literally hundreds of athletes and coaches to build inclusive environments on their teams. Various youth in his area have come out since, telling Anthony that his efforts have been a big part of them finding the courage to be themselves.

That's the domino effect.

It's virtually impossible to erase the fear LGBT people have of coming out, particularly coming out publicly. You can't explain away emotions like fear. What each person can do is inspire courage in others to come out themselves *despite* the fear.

Courage is contagious. One person acting in the face of fear reverberates. Legends are not built by well-to-do trust-fund babies who manage to multiply their father's wealth. Legends are built by courage.

That has been the lasting power of Michael Sam. When he came out, he triggered countless other people to do so as well. He brought the conversation and visibility to places they had never been.

It's not just the stars who have an effect. Every time Jim and I run the coming-out story of a high school or college athlete on *Outsports*, we get at least one more athlete—sometimes three or four—writing to contribute her story. And every story has some of the same core elements:

1. "I was afraid of coming out to my teammates"
2. "When I did come out, my teammates embraced me"
3. "I can't think of a single negative reaction I've gotten from anyone"
4. "I wish I had come out sooner"

Every once in a while someone gets a negative reaction—often from one of his parents or one of her Twitter followers. With very rare exceptions, that fades quickly. In fifteen years, we at *Outsports* have not heard of a single athlete coming out who was roundly rejected by his or her teammates. Every story we have heard—and we have dug deep to find the crap—has been very positive. (The few instances where athletes and coaches are marginalized or pushed out have been based on an interpretation of Christianity that, in the minds of some, seems to mandate outright discrimination.)

When the Supreme Court of the United States legalized same-sex marriage across the country in June 2015, it was the domino effect at work. Because gay couples had stood up publicly and proudly and demanded equality, the Supreme Court was forced to act. Some of these people were men in their twenties and thirties, like Paul Katami and Jeff Zarrillo; others were elderly women like eighty-four-year-old Edie Windsor, who fought for the legal recognition of her marriage to her deceased wife. All of them rejected fear and embraced the fight for equality.

"The power of the closet is what's holding us all back," WNBA player Layshia Clarendon told me. Neither she nor I thinks anyone can shame or guilt people who choose to stay in the closet—everyone has to find her own path. Yet we both know it's only by LGBT people rejecting the naysayers and painting rainbows on their basketball shoes that we truly shine a light through the fear.

"If we all came out," she said, "it would be a lot easier to navigate. I do feel like this is a grassroots movement and the power is in our hands. You have youth knowing they have the power at a much younger age. There are trans high school athletes now. I went to Cal because I knew there were gay people there. It felt right to go there in part because I knew it would be a safe space."

Efforts by non-LGBT people to open sports have helped, no doubt. There have been key policy changes at every level, from youth soccer, where trans inclusion has been at the forefront, to the NFL, where sexual-orientation protection was a cornerstone of the most recent collective bargaining agreement. Education has been eye-opening, with LGBT training programs reaching high school coaches and professional athletes. The visibility of straight athletes talking about their support for LGBT people has helped ease the fear.

All of these pieces have changed the tenor of sports. We've come a long way, but there is only one way to finish the job: everyone needs to come out.

There's only so far that policy and education can move the dial. We can litigate policy and talk to people until we're pink in the face. The only truly transformative piece to our movement's puzzle is the act of coming out.

If every single owner of a professional sports team signed a letter saying he would support a gay player on his team, it would have little effect on the cultures in the locker rooms of those teams and in the lives of LGBT youth.

If every single gay male athlete in pro sports came out publicly—heck, if only a dozen did—it would transform the entire culture in and outside of sports. That's the effect out lesbians have had on the WNBA. The men, sadly, still let fear govern their willingness to live openly.

The time for talking is over. Further policy changes are helpful, but they will have little real-life effect. For people who want to complete the transformation of sports from that of homophobic to inclusive, the only path to true inclusion is to convince people to come out—come out in their own lives, come out on their teams, come out publicly.

I've been told by some activists that it's not their role to convince LGBT athletes to come out. *It's their own private choice,* I hear. Yes, of course it's their choice. And now it's everyone's job to help them make that choice. Speaking engagements, writing blog posts about transphobia—these are no longer enough. They can be marginally helpful, but they are not enough.

We need more waves. We need more tsunamis. If we're going to change the face of sports forever—for the young athletes being born today—we must convince more and more LGBT people in sports to come out and come out publicly.

Fans will not leave them, they will laud them.

Teammates will not harass them, they will hug them.

The media will make them heroes.

They will find a community of LGBT athletes just like them who will make their lives infinitely better.

As I mentioned in this book's introduction, Conner Mertens first contacted me in early 2014. A redshirt freshman kicker for the Willamette University football team, Conner was bisexual and desperately closeted. He had heard the locker room language, "knew" that if you played sports and showered with your teammates you couldn't be a "fag." He was also deeply religious, working with Christian youth groups and helping to lead Bible study with his football team.

Living a lie wasn't Conner's MO, and the weight of his secret got heavier every day. When he finally came out to his team he was too petrified to be in the room, opting for a letter distributed to the players by a coach at a team meeting. The response—now predictable—was overwhelmingly positive and loving. The next day I shared Conner's story on *Outsports*. The dominoes began to fall.

A week later Conner's then-boyfriend, Chandler Whitney, came out to his baseball team and then, again through *Outsports*, came out publicly. His team embraced him.

Mitch Eby, a defensive end on the Chapman University football team, saw Conner's story and reached out to him for help. Within a month he had come out to his team and to the world. Everyone embraced him.

Alec Donovan, a high school state-champion wrestler in New Jersey, tracked down Conner as well. After a year of struggling to tell his father, Alec came out publicly in the middle of his college-recruiting trips. No one backed away from their scholarship offers, and he now wrestles for Cal Poly.

Casey Bethel was a high school baseball and basketball player whose coach told him he could never come out. When he met Conner and Chandler, he found the strength to be his true self. He came out publicly on *Outsports* to a complete embrace by everyone in his life.

Courage is contagious.